THE BEST AMERICAN

Comics 2009

THE BEST AMERICAN

Comics

2009

EDITED *and with an*

INTRODUCTION *by* Charles Burns

JESSICA ABEL & MATT MADDEN,
series editors

HOUGHTON MIFFLIN HARCOURT

BOSTON ▪ NEW YORK   2009

www.hmhbooks.com

ISBN 978-0-618-98965-2

Book design: Robert Overholtzer   Cover design: Michael Kupperman   Endpaper art: Dan Zettwoch

Permissions credits are located on page 333.

Contents

Preface

FLIPPING THROUGH a novel in a bookstore, it's impossible to glean a real sense of the book's content, much less its style or attitude. You'd really need to stand there and read at least a few complete pages. Comics are different this way. Many of us can remember an instance when we took a comic book off the shelf or out of a bin and knew the instant we opened to a random page that we were in love. On any number of occasions, Matt has felt the need to read a comic having only seen the drawing—sometimes after only seeing a single panel excerpted in a review or catalog. At seventeen, Jessica used to "visit" a copy of *Read Yourself Raw* in a local comics store, equally compelled and freaked out by the radical drawings, including some by this book's guest editor, Charles Burns (she eventually bought it, in love at last). Drawing can be powerfully seductive. Some people are attracted by virtuosic rendering or brushwork, others are thrilled by boldly crude outlines, still others get chills from clean colors and crisp, graphic lines. But the instant impression you get from comics is a double-edged sword. Sometimes even the most hardcore and catholic of comics readers come across books whose drawing repels us, provoking distaste or, perhaps worse, indifference. For an artist, how sad to have your work dismissed without even being read! And just because your heavy crosshatching or the way you draw eyes has offended a reader's idiosyncratic taste. Sad but true, because drawing is an essential ingredient of comics and, while there's a lot more to it than that (about which more below), in a real sense—and in contrast to the old cliché about never judging a book by its cover—what you see is what you get. Drawing in comics informs the narrative and expresses an artist's vision: the coolness or nervousness of the lines, the cluttered or sparse nature of the panels, the intensity of distortion or exaggeration, the use of black and white—all of these qualities contribute to the experience of a comic.

However, comics are a *narrative* art form and to truly understand and appreciate them you have to *read* them—drawings, words, panel borders, and all. Only then can you really judge the work fairly. So the despairing cartoonist finds her saviors in the devoted and open-minded readers who overcome an initial dislike of the art to see what she has done *with* the art: How is it used in the service of storytelling? In the act of creating a world? In shading emotion? When we overcome an initial reluctance to read a given comic only to find an unexpected power and richness to the work, *then* we know we are truly readers of comics.

All of us doodle and draw when we are children. But as we grow, most give it up, in a kind of overapplication of the exhortation to "put away childish things." Yet drawing is one of the most basic tools for self-expression available to all of us, and in this way it is closely related to writing. Comics is one of the few places where you'll find these two essential modes of creation so inextricably bound together. In interviews, you'll find many cartoonists describing ways of conceiving the relationship between drawing and writing. Some talk about a calligraphic aspect of drawing for comics, which of course refers to the beauty of sinuous lines and virtuosity, yes, but also likens drawing to writing: the line is meant to be admired for its beauty, but it is primarily a tool of communication. Taking a very different tack, R. Kikuo Johnson (certainly a young master of the "calligraphic" school, one who incidentally gets a shout out in this year's list of notable comics) recently remarked to us that he is concentrating on making his drawing function more like a typographical font: calling as little attention as possible to itself and serving only to communicate language—story—to the reader. Contributor and 2007 guest editor Chris Ware has made similar comments about intending for his art to read as seamlessly as language. He also often likens comics as a whole to sheet music: a schematic diagram that doesn't truly come to life until the reader "performs" the score with his brain.

Drawing brings an incredible richness to comics as well as limitless variety. Of course every novelist and short story writer has her own style, but at a glance, most prose books visually appear very similar, beyond minor variations in font and layout that are likely to pass unnoticed by the majority of readers. In film and video you have the choice of black and white or color, different film stocks and filters, and a growing array of digital tools, yet the root remains recognizable photographic images. Among narrative art forms, only comics (arguably along with its cousin animation) has such a limitless variety of representation.

Individual drawing styles can rarely be reduced to a single philosophy or strategy. Most often, what you see is an organic, constantly evolving dance between a cartoonist's influences, ideas about how comics work, choice of materials, and a combination of native talent and dogged learning. Looking through this volume you'll see a wide variety of types of drawing—in fact, no two stories really look alike, though they may share certain features. Looking at the comics by Gabrielle Bell or CF, you will notice an economy of drawing and composition—clean lines and full-figure blocking in the case of Bell and a thin pencil line in CF—unusual for comics, which are most often inked. A large part of the effect of Tim Hensley's work is due to his pitch-perfect pastiche of postwar teen comics, from line quality to character design to color scheme. We often describe Ben Katchor's work to new readers as looking as if it were scribbled on a diner napkin and tinted with coffee, an effect in tune with the theme of offhand observation of urban life that runs through his work. Dan Zettwoch shares some of the economy and directness of Gabrielle Bell, but in his case it's impossible to separate his drawing from his diagrammatic page layouts, a quality he shares with Chris Ware. Jillian Tamaki's drawing is sensuous and inky, calling attention to the beauty of her brush-strokes while at the same time prioritizing a graphic clarity that makes her comics read as clearly as Ware's or Bell's.

The Best American Comics 2009 represents a selection of the outstanding comics published between September 1, 2007, and August 31, 2008. As series editors, we search out and review comics in as many formats and publications as we can find, from hand-produced mini-comics to individual pamphlet issues to graphic novels and collections to Web comics. Our goal is to put as much interesting and worthwhile material in front of our guest editors as they can stand to read through. This includes not only works that we consider to be excellent by reasonably objective standards, but it certainly also includes comics we have a particular fondness for, as well as left-field choices that may not be our cup of tea but may turn out to be someone else's "best" — and in particular the guest editor's. Guest editors may also seek out material on their own, and they usually do find work that we were unaware of. The guest editor makes the final selections from this large and varied pool of titles. The comics you read in this book aren't the "best" in the sense that they beat out other comics, American Idol–style. What they are is a personally curated selection of top-notch work that reflects just some of the excellence and variety that exists out there, as well as perhaps offering some insight into the tastes and priorities of the guest editor.

This year we were struck by the high level of ambition (and success) of a lot of the comics we reviewed, especially among young cartoonists just starting out, either doing mini-comics or being published by small houses. While many of these works are rough around the edges, they show indications of an entire medium growing beyond its previous boundaries and evolving. Which is not to say that everyone's trying to make the Great American Graphic Novel. There's plenty of inspired humor and silliness out there, as well as engaging examples of genre comics. If you are looking for more evidence of this after finishing the comics in this volume, seek out the books mentioned in the list of notable comics in the back of the book. You will find a wide variety of challenging and enjoyable work by some of tomorrow's best American cartoonists.

And speaking of the list of notable comics, we are pleased to announce that the modern marvel of Internet connectivity has made this a much more useful feature than it has been in the past. Starting with *The Best American Comics 2008,* we have added to the website a page where the list of notable comics is reproduced along with links that should help you to find them. The same will happen with this year's volume, so if you find your comic listed on the website without a link or with a broken one, please contact us with updated information at bestamericancomics@hmhpub.com.

This year's guest editor, Charles Burns, is one of the major icons of comics in the post-underground comix era as well as in our lives as cartoonists. When Matt was making his first, random stabs at educating himself in the world of comics by finding troves of *Heavy Metal* and *National Lampoon* in his dorm storage room, buying used underground comics, and trembling with awe at a copy of *Read Yourself Raw* picked up on a college trip to New York, Charles Burns was one of the first cartoonists to jump out at him, both for his novel combination of horror and humor, as well as for his stylish, masterful brush work. He also came to represent for Matt a model sort of artist, one who works away patiently at his craft, striking a balance between keeping his personal and creative integrity—think of the patience and steadfastness required to spend ten years working on *Black Hole*—while at the same time managing to interact with the world at large and making a distinctive mark on pop culture as a whole, whether on MTV, in advertising, or in toy design. Jessica was a fan early on as well, but really came to love Charles's work when *Black Hole* began appearing, now these many years ago. The change of direction from absurdist, scary stories like his Big Baby work, or el Borbah, to the finely tuned psychological horror of *Black Hole* really knocked her socks off. The sheer beauty of the drawing, juxtaposed with the terror of high school love and served on a platter of genre horror elements, makes *Black Hole* a book for the ages. It was an honor and a pleasure to work with him on this volume.

As we write this preface we are putting Charles's volume to bed, collecting information from the authors, helping get all the necessary files to the art department, and already amassing stacks of books for next year's volume. But we are always hungry for more, so let's go over the submissions guidelines again: comics eligible for consideration must have been published in the eligibility period either on paper on electronically, in English, by a North American author, or one who makes his or her home here. As this 2009 volume hits the shelves, we will have already passed the deadline for the 2010 volume and will be on to collecting for the 2011 volume, whose eligibility window is September 1, 2009, through August 31, 2010. A note about Web comics (and comics on the Web): we do our best to find what's out there, and we rely on friends, blogs, and "best of" lists to track down important work, but we are aware that Web comics is an area that deserves better coverage. Therefore, we'd like to especially encourage you Web cartoonists and publishers to send us submissions either on paper or digitally. Printed submissions can be sent to us at the address below. Digital submissions can be made in the form of a PDF of comics published in the eligibility window with each comic labeled with the exact date it was published online. Or you might make a subselection of what you consider to be your best strips from the year or send a self-contained continuity as long as it appeared in the eligibility period. You can mail a CD of the PDF to us or you can e-mail a download link to bestamericancomics@hmhpub.com.

All comics should be labeled with their release date and contact information and mailed to us at the following address:

Jessica Abel and Matt Madden
Series Editors
The Best American Comics
Houghton Mifflin Harcourt Publishing Co.
215 Park Avenue South
New York, NY 10003

Further information is available on the Best American Comics website: bestamericancomics.com.

We'd like to thank all the people who helped us with this volume, starting with the excellent team at Houghton Mifflin Harcourt: Meagan Stacey, Beth Burleigh Fuller, Christopher Moisan, Sanj Kharbanda, Sasheem Silkiss-Hero, and Ben Steinberg. Thanks also to our great studio assistants Lydia Roberts, Jude Killory, Nate Doyle, and Matt Huynh; to the generous people at publishers and magazines who helped us with art and files: Eric Reynolds, Kim Thompson, Paul Baresh, Tom Devlin, Dan Nadel, Alvin Buenaventura, Aran Church, Helene Silverman, Leigh Stein, Françoise Mouly, Melanie Ryan, Lisa Maione, Randi Geenberg, Dungjai Pungauthaikan, Ted Genoways, and Barb Howson; and of course to all those who helped us find the great work we read this year—among many others, Diana Schutz, Alex Cox, Logan at Quimby's, David at Secret Headquarters, and Chloe Eudaly; and also all the artists and publishers from all over who sent in submissions. We'd like to extend our particular gratitude to Anjali Singh, the best editor one could hope for.

JESSICA ABEL and MATT MADDEN

Introduction

WHAT'S GOOD?

"Flash Gordon" by Alex Raymond is pretty good, but "Flesh Garden" by Harvey Kurtzman and Wally Wood is better. In one form or another I've been searching for "what's good" in the world of comics my entire life, so it made perfect sense for me to agree to edit this edition of *The Best American Comics*. I realize I'm not going to please everyone with my selections—they're obviously a reflection of my personal tastes—but I tried as hard as I could to dig deep in my search for the best, most interesting comics published in the United States and Canada between September 1, 2007, and August 31, 2008. And I really do like Alex Raymond; it's just that Kurtzman and Wood are two artists whose work was indelibly etched on my brain at a tender young age, and they have to be held at least partially responsible for turning me into what I am today.

My father was interested in comics, and there were several books in his collection that I would sit and read endlessly when I was in preschool. I hadn't learned to read yet so I guess I was actually just looking at the pictures, but I remember being completely engrossed by the narratives I was struggling to decipher; it *felt* like reading even if I was inventing a major portion of the stories myself. One series of books in particular took a firm hold of my impressionable mind: the *Mad* comic collections published by Ballantine Books in the late 1950s. They were inexpensive, black and white paperback reprints of the original color comic books, and even though they were supposed to be humorous stories—parodies of popular movies, books, and television shows—there was something dark and forbidding about them: a glimpse into a complex, adult world that I found both intriguing and repulsive. You have to keep in mind that Kurtzman's *Mad* comics were originally published by EC Comics, the same publisher responsible for such childhood favorites as *Tales from the Crypt* and *Weird Science,* and as a result, some of the creepy atmosphere found in their horror and science fiction comics definitely seeped into the pages of *Mad.*

Not only did I spend an inordinate amount of time poring over the pages of *Mad* but I had an early epiphany when I discovered my father drawing a copy of three panels from "Flesh Garden." I have no idea what his motivation was, but he had always been enthusiastic about hobbies of every kind: wood carving, model building, painting lead soldiers, stamp and coin collecting, building model railroads, sketching, water coloring and . . . cartooning. Unfortunately, the original he created seems to be lost forever, but to my eyes it was an amazing piece of work. Even though I recognized the fact that it looked like a slightly distorted version of Wally Wood's artwork, it was amazingly precise—especially the lettering. It was at that moment I realized comic books were actually drawn by human hands—I had proof right there in front of me.

Another book from my father's collection that I studied carefully was *A Complete Guide to Professional Cartooning* by Gene Byrnes. In addition to the standard how-to lessons on the basics of cartooning, there were chapters devoted to a wide array of talented artists that I don't normally associate with commercial cartooning, such as Daumier, Boris Artzybasheff, and Heinrich Kley. There were a few sleepless nights when I wished I could excise from my mind a drawing by Daumier that depicted a group of animated corpses—he sure as hell knew how to create potent images, but that one in particular gave me endless nightmares. Looking at it again from an adult perspective, I understand why the author explains that the drawing "has seldom been published because of its gruesomeness."

No doubt I'm giving the impression that everything I looked at as a preschooler was dark and creepy (or at least made me *feel* dark and creepy) but nothing could be further from the truth. One of the highlights of life at that time was receiving a copy of Tintin in *The Secret of the Unicorn* by Hergé. Golden Press published six volumes of *The Adventures of Tintin* in the late '50s and early '60s, but apparently they didn't really catch on with an American audience—I have yet to meet another American cartoonist of my generation who grew up reading them. It's difficult to express the impression that first Tintin book made on me, but it was the perfect comic as far as I was concerned—Hergé had created a unique, beautifully rendered world that I could step into and spend hours wandering around. When I found out it was only one in a whole series of books, I made it abundantly clear to my parents that I absolutely *had* to have them all; luckily, they complied.

One of the intriguing but frustrating parts of reading the Tintin series was the fact that I could get my hands on only six of them. The back cover of each book listed the titles that were available from Golden Press, along with the aggravating blurb: "Watch for additional new titles." I was watching, I really was, but in the meantime there were abundant clues to Tintin's other adventures in the back cover illustration and in the gallery of character portraits found on the endpapers. One image in particular fueled my imagination: a crumbling castle seen off on the horizon of the weirdly surreal back cover landscape (where *were* they and what was that bulbous red and white mushroom doing there?). I wanted to get out to that island *so* bad, or at least be transported there through another Tintin book, but I was in for a long wait. Needless to say, by the time I found a British translation of *The Black Island* in the early '70s, it was too late; it was a perfectly good book, but nothing could live up to the story I had dreamed up as a kid.

We moved around a lot when I was growing up, and in each new location I did my best to uncover a source of comics—pestering my parents and friends, and scouring the local drugstores and supermarkets. I took what I could find—usually fairly pedestrian superhero comics like *Batman* and *Superman*—but every once in a while, my search would yield something intriguing. I found a copy of *Spider-Man #6* in a well-read stack of comics I'd traded with a friend, and there was something about the artwork and the characters that I connected with immediately. It quickly became my comic of choice. I read all of the early issues drawn by Steve Ditko and stayed around when John "Ring-A-Ding" Romita took over the artwork. I didn't realize at the time that I was more interested in the day-to-day life of Peter Parker than the exploits of his alter ego Spider-Man—in some ways it was a carefully disguised romance comic, a soap opera for prepubescent boys.

After our family moved to Seattle in the mid '60s, I discovered Zoph's—a local Mom and Pop drugstore that carried just about every comic published in America. I diligently made weekly pilgrimages there and slowly amassed a huge collection of titles like *The Fantastic Four, The Hulk, Daredevil, Nick Fury: Agent of S.H.I.E.L.D.*—just about anything with good art and a decent story. I stuck with it for years, but by the time I reached eighth grade, my interest in mainstream superhero comics finally started to wane. I was looking for something else—something more . . . adult. Luckily for me, underground comix showed up.

I was introduced to them one day at Nathan Eckstein Junior High School, when Steve Paulkin stopped me in the hall and said, "Hey, Burns, you like comics, right? Well, wait till you see *Zap*. My brother has a copy and the stories are really, really dirty." He was right; some of them were really, really dirty ("What's he *doing* to her?"), but there was more to them than that; they were a key element in the hippie youth culture I was just beginning to discover (but a little too young to participate in), along with black-light posters, underground newspapers, and head shops. In less than a year I switched from drawing superhero parodies to thinly disguised rip-offs of Robert Crumb, Rick Griffin, and Victor Moscoso (S. Clay Wilson was a little too hardcore for me). I got into deep trouble in ninth grade when it was discovered that my page of comics titled "Handie Comics" (spelling error or artistic license?) published in *The Elm* (the Eckstein literary magazine) not only contained hidden "swear words," but I'd also copied other artists' work and called it my own. The concept of creating and publishing original work was sacred to the English teacher that edited the magazine, but it was one that had never really crossed my mind up until then.

By the time I reached high school, the "hippie dream" had started to fade, the revolution wasn't showing signs of coming anytime soon, and I'd become focused on creating comics that weren't quite so directly derivative of Crumb and his cohorts. I had vague ideas about making "art" comics—something I didn't really have a definition for other than creating pieces that didn't follow any rules other than "looking" like comics. I'd found bits of information in books like *A History of the Comic Strip* by Couperie and Horn and *The Penguin Book of Comics* by Perry and Aldridge about artists who used comic imagery or references in their art, and I think I subconsciously appropriated some of their "strategies." A blurry reproduction of "Tricky Cad," where the artist reassembled and collaged panels taken from Dick Tracy was particularly intriguing—years later I'd recognize a similar postmodern approach to comics in Art Spiegelman's "The Malpractice Suite."

I'd always searched through used bookstores for back issues of comics and magazines, but one day while wandering through the Pike Place Market in downtown Seattle, I discovered that a small corner of one of my regular haunts had been converted into a makeshift comic book store. The glass display cases were filled with early issues of *Batman, Superman,* and titles I'd never seen before outside the pages of books like Jules Feiffer's *The Great Comic Book Heroes*. These expensive collectors' items were out of reach and well out of my price range, but the more affordable back issues were placed in bins with their jacked-up prices penciled in on the inside page. After long deliberation, for three dollars I bought a beat-up copy of *Jungle Comics* published by Fiction House way back in 1949. The stories were pretty crummy, but the art was great—lots of scantily clad girls in leopard-skin outfits and plenty of excessively violent imagery—the kind of comics that Fredric Wertham had warned the parents of America about in his book, *Seduction of the Innocent,* and the kind I had a predilection for. I found that if I stayed away from the more popular "collectible" titles and wasn't concerned about their condition, there were plenty of old, pre-code crime, jungle, and romance comics that I could afford.

Even after I went off to college to study "fine art," I continued drawing my comics on the side. I jumped around from school to school because I had no idea what I wanted to do, but everywhere I went, I'd make an attempt to get my work published in the school paper. *The Daily* of the University of Washington wasn't interested (maybe because I made the mistake of telling the editor how crappy I thought their comics were) but there was a short run of my comic, "Crypto Wanderlust Comics," at Central Washington State College, and by the time I wound up at The Evergreen State College in 1976, I was having work published regularly in their student-run paper, the *Cooper Point Journal.* The school mascot was a geoduck (look it up), there were no grades and no sports teams, Lynda Barry ran the art gallery (and gave me my first show), and Matt Groening edited the paper. I was at the right place at the right time.

Lynda and Matt would eventually go on to become two of the most famous American cartoonists of my generation, but it wasn't until 1981 that I met a "real" cartoonist—Art Spiegelman. He coedited *RAW* magazine with his wife Françoise Mouly, and after mailing them photocopies of my comics, I was invited to come up to New York and show them more. I'd had plenty of teachers and friends look at my comics over the years, but Art was the first person I'd met who really seemed to understand what I was getting at. We sat down in their loft and Art proceeded to slowly look though my stack of work. When I say "slowly," I mean he looked at each piece a long, long time; *so* long that at some point I nervously started to blurt out an explanation of the page he was examining, but was quickly cut off: "Wait. That's against the rules. You should never have to explain your work." And he was right. After that, we got along just fine.

Art and Françoise not only agreed to publish my comics in Raw, but they also were instrumental in helping me navigate the early stages of my career with advice, practical information, and moral support. I would come up to visit them and we would sit and drink coffee and talk comics. As we talked, Art would periodically jump up to grab a book by some artist I'd never heard of—an hour later, the coffee table would be piled high with the most amazing books on the planet. It was the final stage of my formal education; it was where I discovered artists like Joost Swarte, Kaz, Pascal Doury, Ever Meulen, Mark Beyer, Jacques Tardi—the list is endless. After our meetings, I'd drive my decaying Buick Skylark back to Philadelphia with my creative batteries charged enough to continue on in my struggle to become a "real" cartoonist.

For the most part, the artists in this book were already well known to me—that's just the way it works; these days, if you're a reasonably talented cartoonist, it's hard to stay under the radar for long. Out of the thirty-six pieces chosen for this book, twenty cartoonists have had their work published in at least one of the three previous editions of *Best American Comics*, and only four were previously unknown to me. As I've tried to explain, I've always kept my eyes open for new work so the fact that I made any discoveries at all was encouraging to me—a sign that my chosen medium is alive and well and my list of "what's good" is still growing.

CHARLES BURNS

THE BEST AMERICAN

Comics 2009

TIM HENSLEY

REALLY? OH, IF ONLY I WERE ABLE TO PLANT MY LIPS ON ONE. THERE'S NO TELLING HOW DEMONSTRATIVELY GRATEFUL I'D BE!

YOU SEE, I'VE ALWAYS DREAMED OF BEING UP THERE BELTING OUT TO THE BLEACHERS.

I WANT TO BE A CONDUIT FOR THE TENDER FEELINGS A PEOPLE HAVE FOR THEIR HOMELAND.

I WANT TO BE UP ON THE PITCHER'S MOUND WITH A P.A.

THOSE FELLAS WILL JUST HAVE TO WAIT TO CHEER FOR THE PIGSKIN UNTIL RESPECTS ARE PAID.

IF THEY GOT A CAP ON, THEY BETTER LOSE IT. IF THEY'RE CHEWING GUM, THEY BETTER SPIT IT OUT.

4

DANIEL CLOWES

SOMETIMES A CRITIC HAS TO MAKE SOME VERY TOUGH DECISIONS. HERE I HAD WRITTEN A DEVASTATING ATTACK, BUT SOME NAGGING VESTIGE OF GUILT KEPT ME FROM UPLOADING IT. WAS HE TELLING THE TRUTH WITH HIS LITTLE EXCUSE? DID IT MATTER?

ELLEN USED TO MAKE FUN OF MY TASTE IN MOVIES. SHE SAID I WAS A "ROMANTIC SAP" WHO PREFERRED ART CREATED BY FOCUS GROUPS AND COMMITTEES OVER THE IDIOSYNCRATIC NUANCE OF A SINGULAR VOICE. AND OF COURSE SHE WAS RIGHT.

ALL I CAN SAY IS THAT SHE CRIED AT THE END OF TITANIC AND I FELL ASLEEP DURING LE MÉPRIS.

I BELIEVE IN THE TRANSFORMATIVE POWER OF CINEMA. IT IS ONLY THROUGH THIS SHARED DREAM-EXPERIENCE THAT WE CAN TRANSCEND THE OPPRESSIVE MINUTIAE OF DAILY EXISTENCE AND FIND SOME SPIRITUAL CONNECTION IN THE DEEPER REALITY OF OUR MUTUAL DESIRE.

HOW OFTEN HAVE WE WATCHED A MOVIE AND WISHED WE COULD FEEL THOSE EMOTIONS IN OUR REAL LIVES? BUT WHAT'S STOPPING US? WHY CAN'T WE REJECT THE MUNDANE AND EMBRACE THE POSSIBILITIES OFFERED BY A CINEMA OF PLURALISTIC WISH-FULFILLMENT?

UM, WE KIND OF HAVE THIS NEW POLICY THAT YOU'RE NOT SUPPOSED TO SIT AT A TABLE FOR MORE THAN TWO HOURS.

WHEN ELLEN FINALLY LEFT, SHE SAID SHE FELT AS THOUGH SHE DIDN'T EVEN KNOW ME. SHE SAID I LIVED ENTIRELY INSIDE MY OWN HEAD. I CAN SEE HER POINT, AND I OFTEN WONDER IF SHE'S EVER SEEN MY SITE. THEN SHE'D KNOW THE REAL ME.

AND SO I HIT THE UPLOAD BUTTON AND LAUNCHED FIFTY UNSTOPPABLE MEGATONS OF JUSTIN DAMIANO INTO THE ETHER.

DC '05

KAZ

DOUG ALLEN

ALINE KOMINSKY-CRUMB

ROBERT CRUMB AND ALINE KOMINSKY-CRUMB

MICHAEL KUPPERMAN

Hey! Remember the 70s? Tuna Mac'n'Cheese, Flashing Mags, and those TV cops Twain & Einstein! Join us now for some selections from their comic book adventures.

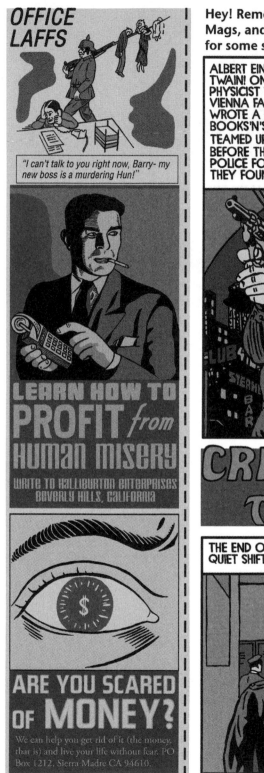

SUDDENLY THE CHIEF ENTERS!

HEY, BOYS! WHATTYA THINK OF MY NEW TARZAN GETUP?

CHIEF, PLEASE PUT ON THE CHIEF CLOTHES AGAIN, WILLYA? SICK IT'S MAKING ME!

I ALSO AM DISGUSTED!

COMMANDER

SOON—

ALRIGHT, SO I PUT MY UNIFORM BACK ON— WHY AREN'T I BEING REWARDED WITH SMILES?

IT WAS UNPROFESSIONAL!

TOMORROW'S MY DAY OFF— I'M GOING TO HIDE IN A BOX, AND WAIT FOR SOMEONE TO STEAL ME!

AND I'LL SHOW UP TOO, PROBABLY

HMM. HMM. DAY OFF, HIDE IN BOX. IT'S SO CRAZY IT JUST MIGHT WORK.

THEN WE BUST THE SUCKER!

ASK SWELLY

Dear Swelly,
The other day I mistakenly drank while standing in a freshly varnished storeroom. When I came to, my roommate Clive, who looks like a dressed-up fish, was standing in the doorway.

"Wuh... I had such an awful bump on my head." I said. "So... what's happening?"
"Was I in your dream?" he asked.
"Yeah, you were... you were delivering weird, non-sensical gossip in a shrill, unpleasant voice."
"Was I? Then hold on to your bits, love." he smirked.

"Shirley Pablum *has been loining it up with* Jason Rotunda, *despite his being fictional and a rotunda.*
Who was out the other night at super-hot club Dunghole until 9:30 the following evening? Not super-hot Paul Giamatti, who got very angry when he found us lurking in his bushes... Spotted at Replica: Lindsay Lohan *partying with* The Human Sneeze...*Hot new sensation* Celery Tomato *has been spotted incorporating himself, in contravention of several local regulations.*

The Human Sneeze

"The other day I opened up a banana and there were raisins in it. Only in this town, kids, only in this town...
This is Oscar Wilde IV, *saying don't be tiresome! I hate it when people are tiresome."*

DAN ZETTWOCH

SPIRIT DUPLICATOR

USING WHAT WE CALLED the **Ditto** a.k.a. the "SPIRIT DUPLICATOR"

WHEN the 80's ROLLED AROUND, St. BART's CONGREGATION WAS RAPIDLY SHRINKING—DYING OFF or MOVING ON—BUT I STILL TRIED TO GIVE the DIE-HARDS PLENTY OF BANG for their BUCK.

SMALLER, MORE ECONOMICAL MACHINE

2-PLY SPIRIT MASTER: FIRST SHEET TYPED or DRAWN ON, SECOND SHEET COATED IN COLORED WAX AND IMPRINTED WITH DESIGN.

IT WAS BASICALLY the SAME PROCESS AS WITH the MIMEO STENCIL EXCEPT I COULD ATTACH MULTIPLE SPIRIT MASTERS to the DRUM FOR A 2-COLOR EFFECT.

ZIP

PROPYL

FOR the WAXY MASTER to MAKE AN IMPRINT, the FRESH PAPER HAD TO BE SOAKED WITH A SUPER-TOXIC SOLVENT.

AND THERE'D YOU HAVE IT, THAT CLASSIC PURPLE DITTO SHEET! UNFORTUNATELY, the BULLETIN WAS DOWN TO A COUPLE OF FOLDED SHEETS, and I WAS FORCED TO SHARE REAL ESTATE WITH BIRTHDAYS and ANNOUNCEMENTS. THE NEW VESTRY WAS NOT REALLY BEHIND ME IN **1982**

TURNS OUT THIS STUFF WAS REALLY BAD FOR US.

BIRTHDAYS
...oaridge 68
...edbud 82
...biegott 79
... 85
...ster 49
...ck

SUNDAY SERVICES
Morning Service 8:00
Sunday School 9:30
Sunday School (Adults) 9:30
Holy Eucharist &
...ermon 10:45
... Service 6:00

AND THEY WERE TRYING TO SHAPE UP the ACOLYTES, TOO

THIS IS A MOTIF I USED EVERY ONCE IN A WHILE, TOO— "GOOFUS" AND "GALLANT"

I HAD TO RE-TYPE the SUNDAY SCHEDULE and RE-TRACE this LITTLE DRAWING of the CHURCH EVERY WEEK on the MASTER STENCIL.

DON'Ts

DOs

ALTAR

ALTAR

I RIPPED IT OFF FROM HIGHLIGHTS MAGAZINE. (MY DAUGHTERS HAD A SUBSCRIPTION.)

A. Chewing gum
B. Dripping wax
C. Incorrect candle-lighting sequence
D. Unprofessional processional
E. Whoopie Cushion
F. Not parti-cipating in song
G. White Sneakers

A. Participating in Song
B. Steady and upright
C. Correct candle-lighting sequence
D. professional
...

THE BAD PART ABOUT the DITTO's OUTPUT — IN ADDITION TO BEING REALLY FOUL-SMELLING — WAS THAT EACH PRINT GOT WORSE AND WORSE AS YOU WENT ON. LUCKILY WE ONLY HAD TO MAKE A COUPLE HUNDRED.

TO BE HONEST, I ALWAYS LIKED 'GOOFUS' BETTER!

"TERRY"ble TORCHBEARER

"CARRIE"ful CRUCIFER

ST. BARTHOLOMEW'S EPISCOPAL   St. LOUIS, MISSOURI   APRIL 4, 1982

43

3.

The Company

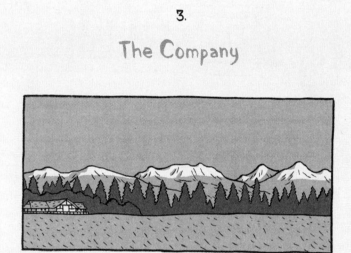

One Wednesday afternoon in Los Angeles, some years ago, Miles Anderson found himself at the beach, watching the waves roll in and smoking a cigarette.

Miles was a television producer, and would have been at his desk or in a meeting if a string of disasters hadn't befallen him that day.

Things had started off well enough. Miles was having an affair with a girl from the office, and had arranged to meet her in a hotel that was too run-down for there to be any danger of meeting someone he knew.

Things only got worse from there... with the phone call from his boss...

...About the big meeting with a Vegas outfit called Casinotron... They were trying to get their hands on Poker TV, the secret project in the works at Miles' company.

The idea of Poker TV was to let you join poker games anywhere in the world, over a regular TV set.

You'd have the whole casino experience without ever getting off the sofa...

Casinotron wanted to install Poker TV in every motel west of the Mississippi.

It would be a gold mine... All those people stuck in the middle of nowhere with nothing to do...

In fact, Casinotron was so keen to get started they had agreed to buy the whole company.

With his payoff, Miles' boss was going on a round-the-world cruise with his beautiful Filipina Secretary.

Everybody else was being fired. Miles would need to come and collect his things sometime, but there was no hurry.

ADRIAN TOMINE

MAY 23, 1978. MIDAFTERNOON. I AM THE ONLY CUSTOMER.

A BELL ON THE FRONT DOOR RINGS
AS SOMEONE ENTERS.

A MAN NIMBLY TWIRLS HIMSELF BEHIND THE COUNTER
AND OVER TO THE REGISTER.

THAT TURNED OUT TO BE A DISTINCTIVELY LAZLO-LIKE
DIP AND TWIRL HE'D DO.

NOW THAT I THINK ABOUT IT, HE WAS PROBABLY HIGH. DOES IT MATTER?

76

HE'S KIND OF CUTE FOR AN OLD GUY, WHICH, I FIND OUT LATER, IS THIRTY-SEVEN, ANCIENT.

WHEN HE SAYS THIS, HIS EYES TAKE ON A DECIDED SLANT AND HIS WISPY MUSTACHE SEEMS A BIT FU MANCHU-ISH.

MAKING HIMSELF LOOK CHINESE AT WILL, I FIND OUT LATER, IS JUST ONE OF HIS TALENTS.

I'D SCRAPED UP ENOUGH CHANGE TO BUY A CUP OF COFFEE.

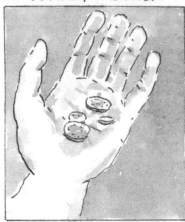

I'D WALKED THE SIX BLOCKS FROM SCHOOL.

IT FELT GOOD TO GET OUT OF THERE, AWAY FROM THE NEWS I'D GOTTEN, AWAY FROM ART, OUT INTO THE FRESH AIR.

I'D DECIDED NOT TO GO TO DAVE'S, AN UNTOUCHED MONUMENT OF A 1950'S DINER.

I HAVE FILLED SKETCHBOOK AFTER SKETCHBOOK WITH DRAWINGS OF THE CUSTOMERS HERE, THEIR FAT BUTTS CRAWLING OVER THE EDGE OF THE STOOLS. I HAVE DRAWN THE COFFEE POTS...

SECURE IN THEIR BUNN-O-MATIC STATIONS...

I HAVE DRAWN THE NAPKIN DISPENSERS...

AND I HAVE DRAWN THE WAITRESSES.

I ADMIRE THE WAITRESSES AT DAVE'S, BECAUSE THEY ARE NO-SHIT GALS WITH NAMES LIKE BEA AND MYRNA, WOMEN WHO KNOW ABOUT REAL LIFE, NOT LIKE ME, A SNIVELING, PRIVILEGED GIRL WHO HAS DONE NOTHING BUT DRAW, REPEATEDLY, MANY BUS INTERIORS, NUMEROUS BUS DEPOTS, AND COUNTLESS COFFEE SHOPS IN ORDER TO TRY TO PIN DOWN REAL LIFE.

I SHOULD ALSO ADD THAT I HAVE SPENT TOO MUCH TIME ALONE IN MY ROOM WITH TOM WAITS ALBUMS.

SHE'S UP AGAINST THE REGISTER WITH AN APRON AND A SPATULA...

THESE WAITRESSES ARE NOT DISPOSED TO THINK KINDLY OF ME. ART STUDENTS ARE NOT GOOD TIPPERS.

I NEED SOMETHING NEW.

I GET TO THIS PLACE. I'D ASSUMED IT WAS AN ABANDONED CHINESE RESTAURANT.

IMPERIAL CAFE
CHINESE AMERICAN
LUNCH · DINNER

OPEN

BUT THE SIGN SAYS "OPEN."

THE MINUTE I OPEN THE FRONT DOOR, THE SMELL OF COFFEE IS OVERWHELMING AND NARCOTIC,

TO MY SURPRISE, INSTEAD OF A TEENY, FACTORY-SEALED PLASTIC CONTAINER OF NON-DAIRY PRODUCT LIKE THEY GIVE YOU AT DAVE'S...

SHE GIVES ME A TINY BEAKER OF REAL CREAM ALONG WITH MY COFFEE.

THE FLAVOR IS RICH. ROUND. THREE-DIMENSIONAL, NOTHING LIKE THE USUAL THIN, GRAY COFFEE SHOP FARE. IT HARDLY WASHES OVER MY TONGUE BEFORE I GET A JOLT OF THAT CAFFEINE OPTIMISM, A RAY OF SUNSHINE FLOODING THE INSIDE OF MY BRAIN. LIFE LOOKS GOOD MY HEART IS BEATING FASTER.

EVEN THOUGH I TOLD MYSELF I WOULDN'T, I PULL MY SKETCHBOOK OUT OF MY BACKPACK AND GET OUT MY FOUNTAIN PEN. I BEGIN TO DRAW THE WHOLE TABLEAU HERE.

AND NOW THIS GUY WHO IS NOT CHINESE, WHO HAS TWIRLED IN WITH THE CHINESE PARSLEY, PLOPS DOWN ON THE SEAT NEXT TO ME.

I INSTANTLY RECOGNIZE THE COMIC, DRUGGY ALTER EGO, ONE OF THOSE THINGS PEOPLE, ANYWHERE FROM TWO TO TWENTY YEARS OLDER THAN ME LIKE TO DO, GIVE THEMSELVES SILLY ALIASES:

THE SUBTEXT IS THE CONCEIT THAT THEY ARE ACTUALLY SO SUBVERSIVE AND DANGEROUS (SOMETHING TO DO WITH DRUGS OR REVOLUTION) THAT THEY MUST TRAVEL UNDER ASSUMED NAMES. I MISSED THE COUNTERCULTURAL BOAT BY BEING JUST A LITTLE TOO YOUNG. I USED TO REGRET THAT. THE LAST COUPLE OF YEARS, THOUGH, THE WHOLE HIPPIE THING HAS STARTED TO GET ON MY NERVES.

LAZLO THROWS BACK HIS HEAD AND CACKLES. HE HAS SUCH A WELCOMING LAUGH.

HAHAHAHAHAHA!

IT IS A BUBBLING FOUNTAIN OF ENTRE-NOUS.

HE CERTAINLY IS FORTH-COMING, A SWITCH FROM THE BROODING, WILLFULLY OBLIQUE BOYS WHO'VE BEEN DRIVING ME CRAZY FOR THE LAST THREE YEARS OF ART SCHOOL. ABRUPTLY, I BLURT OUT:

DO YOU HAVE A GIRLFRIEND?

I AM LONELY AND LUMPISH. I LACK ANY INSTINCT FOR THE FEMALE MYSTERY.

THERE IS ONLY THE SMALLEST AWKWARD HALF-BEAT.

OH, SWEETIE,

I'VE GOT A WIFE AND KIDS. FOUR.

BUT I'M FLATTERED THAT YOU ASK.

HE PICKS UP MY SKETCHBOOK AGAIN.

ALRIGHT!

THE IMPERIAL ACHIEVES IMMORTALITY AT LAST!

I GET AN IDEA. THIS IS ONE OF THOSE MINGY, FREELOADING THINGS I HAVE LEARNED TO DO AS A STUDENT.

DO YOU THINK I COULD TRADE THIS DRAWING FOR A MEAL?

SURE, HON. I THINK WE COULD SWING THAT.

CARE FOR A TOUR OF THE KITCHEN?

...SAYS LAZLO, CHANGING MY IDENTITY IN AN INSTANT.

ALL OF THIS SEEMS SO FAMILIAR THAT I FIND MYSELF TRYING TO REMEMBER WHERE AND WHEN I MET THESE PEOPLE. IT SEEMS LIKE WE'VE ALREADY KNOWN EACH OTHER FOR YEARS...

I AM TRYING TO FIGURE OUT HOW TO STICK AROUND, BUT...

I AM REMINDED THAT THESE PEOPLE, UNLIKE ME, ARE ACTUALLY WORKING.

Synopsis
MY PAST KEEPS
COMING BACK TO ME

PORTRAIT OF THE ARTIST AS A YOUNG % ⑥ ? ☆ !

Washington Heights, nyc. ca.1952

SIGH —MEANWHILE, IN WIMBLEDON, TIGER WOODS WINS THE SILVER CUP! ...and tennis, of course!

The Hell with it! In a log cabin, somewhere on Mars. OH LENI! YES, CARLOS! YES! YES! A *Triumph of the Will* DVD droned in the background while they climaxed together.

Crumpled pages of his memoir littered the floor. LUCINDA! Maybe fiction was invented so your spouse wouldn't kill you...

...but fiction always struck him like playing tennis without a net!

FORM AND CONTENT

"AND SO, LIFE IS RECKONED AS NOTHING. HABITUATION DEVOURS WORKS, CLOTHES, FURNITURE, ONE'S WIFE. AND THE FEAR OF WAR...

AND ART EXISTS THAT ONE MAY RECOVER THE SENSATION OF LIFE: IT EXISTS TO MAKE ONE FEEL THINGS, TO MAKE THE STONE STONY.

THE PURPOSE OF ART IS TO IMPART THE SENSATION OF THINGS AS THEY ARE PERCEIVED AND NOT AS THEY ARE KNOWN.

THE TECHNIQUE OF ART IS TO MAKE OBJECTS 'UNFAMILIAR,' TO MAKE FORMS DIFFICULT, TO INCREASE THE DIFFICULTY AND LENGTH OF PERCEPTION...

BECAUSE THE PROCESS OF PERCEPTION IS AN AESTHETIC END IN ITSELF AND MUST BE PROLONGED,

PTUI!

ART IS A WAY OF EXPERIENCING THE *ARTFULNESS* OF AN OBJECT: THE OBJECT IS NOT IMPORTANT." —Victor Shklovsky, "Art as Technique." 1917

92

RON REGÉ JR.

GABRIELLE BELL

GARY PANTER

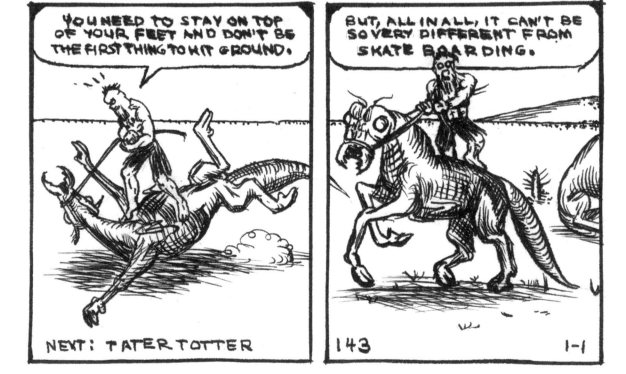

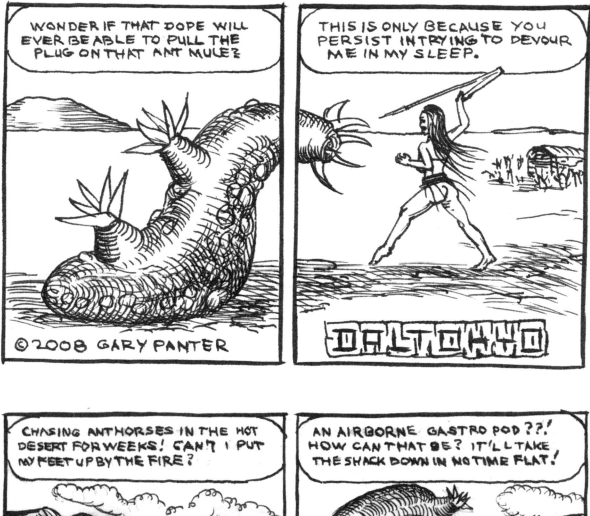

Disinfected Youth

A CHILD IDLY LICKS A MAHOGANY BANISTER.

RAPHAEL!

DON'T WORRY, EVERYTHING IN OUR HOME IS IMPREGNATED OR COATED WITH A POWERFUL ANTI-MICROBIAL AGENT.

TREATED WITH MICRO MORT 99

IT DISRUPTS THE FUNCTION AND GROWTH OF ALL BACTERIA. SHOULD WE CHOOSE TO, WE COULD EAT OUR DINNER DIRECTLY OFF THE FLOOR.

THOSE OBJECTS ONCE FORBIDDEN TO THE HUMAN TONGUE ARE NOW BACTERIA-FREE.

DOORKNOBS, SWITCH PLATES, KEYBOARDS, TOYS, TAPS, AND TABLES.

TRASH BAGS, TABLES, WALL-COVERINGS, AND SOCKS.

TO RESTORE THE NORMAL BALANCE OF MICROBIAL LIFE WITHIN THEIR BODIES, SOME YOUNG PEOPLE SUCK "COCCI DROPS."

HARD CANDIES CONTAINING AN ASSORTMENT OF PATHOGENIC AND NONPATHOGENIC BACTERIA.

THE CANDIES ARE MANUFACTURED IN A SQUALID FACTORY ON SPIRILLA AVENUE.

COCCI CANDY

THE VATS OF MOLTEN SUGAR ARE OPEN TO DUST, INSECTS, AND RODENT EXCREMENT.

EACH HARDENED DROP IS FED INTO A GRIME-ENCRUSTED MACHINE.

NARROW ROLLS OF CELLOPHANE AND WAX PAPER ARE STORED ON A FILTHY LOADING DOCK.

NO PARKING

THE PAPER FLOWS INTO THE TWISTING TURRET, WHERE IT'S CUT TO AN EXACT SIZE BY A DIRTY BLADE.

COCCI DROPS

A PAIR OF SOILED MECHANICAL FINGERS TWIST THE ENDS CLOSED.

NO THANKS. MY IMMUNE SYSTEM IS VERY WEAK.

BEN KATCHOR

Gravel Migration

The Wide Riders

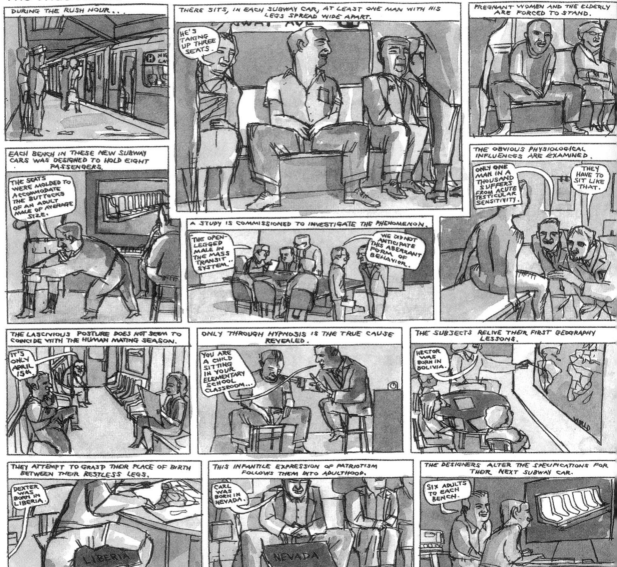

JERRY MORIARTY

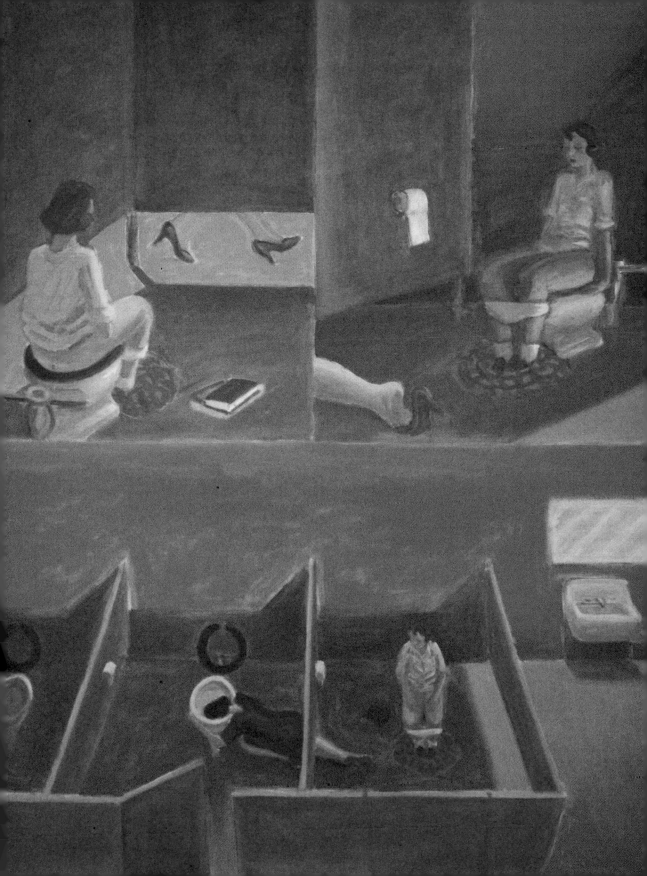

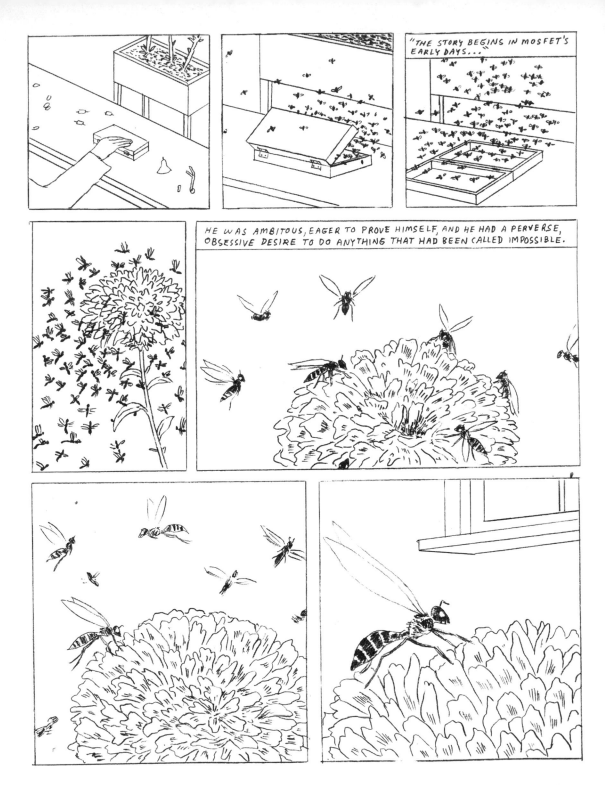

"THE STORY BEGINS IN MOSFET'S EARLY DAYS..."

HE WAS AMBITOUS, EAGER TO PROVE HIMSELF, AND HE HAD A PERVERSE, OBSESSIVE DESIRE TO DO ANYTHING THAT HAD BEEN CALLED IMPOSSIBLE.

MOSFET LABORED ENDLESSLY IN HIS MAGICAL LABORATORY.

IT WAS A PLACE WHERE THE ASSUMPTIONS OF THE OUTSIDE WORLD WERE BROUGHT TO TASK AND ANNIHILATED.

A WARLOCK LIKE MOSFET IS ALWAYS INTERESTED IN DOING THE IMPOSSIBLE, EVEN AT THE COST OF BECOMING DEEPLY PERVERSE. HE COULD NOT HELP BUT BECOME ATTRACTED TO THE DEPRAVED IDEA OF DEATH-REVERSAL.

WHEN MOSFET HAD GONE AS FAR AS HE COULD IN THE LAB, HE WOULD GO OUTSIDE AND WANDER.

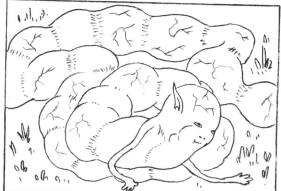

133

THE GAS HAD A STRANGE HEAVY SMELL, MAGNETIC AND REPULSIVE AT ONCE... IT MADE MOSFET'S INSIDES TINGLE LIKE OZONE...

MOSFET COLLECTED THE GAS & FUNNELED IT INTO A CHAMBER WITH CORPSES.

THEY CHANGED WHEN SHOCKED WITH PLAIN ELECTRICITY.

ON INTUITION, MOSFET BURIED THESE "SEEDS" IN THE GROUND OUTSIDE.

THE MECHTEMBRE SOON FOUND THEIR WAY TO MOSFET'S LAB...

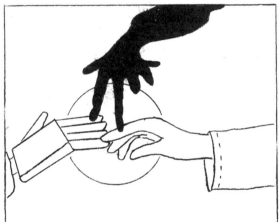

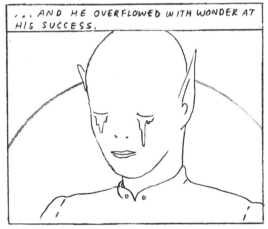

...AND HE OVERFLOWED WITH WONDER AT HIS SUCCESS.

THEY HAD DRAGGED A DEAD BODY THEY FOUND TO HIS LAB. THEY KNEW MOSFET COULD MAKE MORE OF THEIR KIND FROM THE CORRUPTING FLESH...

THIS HE DID.

LO_ BOT O M Y~ He art

DAVID SANDLIN

145

TEN YEARS LATER, 3518,
STAN PLUGS INTO HIS
HELNET AND FINDS
A GALLERY OF
GALACTIC-FUNNEL-INSPIRED
ARTWORK BY
DON DAK.

WHAT AN UNUSUAL WAY OF
VIEWING A GALACTIC FUNNEL!
SEEN FROM ABOVE. NOT CONE-
SHAPED OR 3-DIMENSIONAL
AT ALL! <u>FLAT</u>! A CIRCLE!

SEPTEMBER, 3508
A SIX YEAR-OLD
STAN SMART
FIRST SEES THE
GALACTIC FUNNELS
ON A HOLIDAY TRIP
WITH HIS PARENTS.

by dash shaw, september 2007

SOON:

WORK BY STAN SMART:

STAN SMART'S FAVORITE ARTIST, DON DAK:

DON DAK REPRODUCTION:

STAN SMART ORIGINAL:

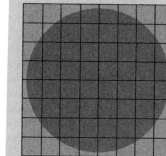

MARVELOUS, STAN! IT REALLY LOOKS LIKE A DON DAK ORIGINAL! HOW DID YOU EVER THINK OF A GALACTIC FUNNEL THIS WAY?

3520: STAN ENTERS THE MARTIAN CRAFT SCHOOL TO STUDY UNDER DON DAK.

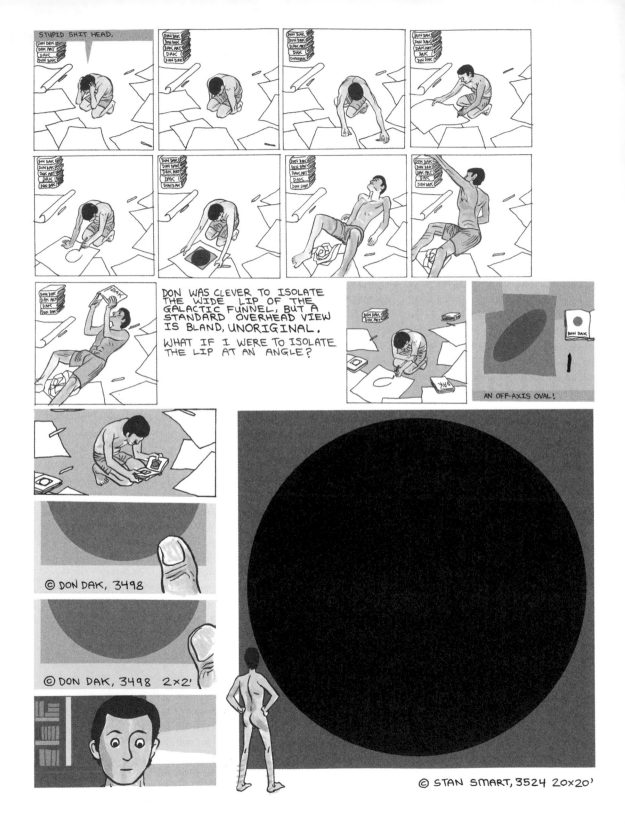

© STAN SMART, 3524 20×20'

STAN SMART SHOWS SLIDES,
DISCUSSES RECENT WORK.

4·8·3529   SECTOR 6B-9

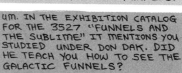

I ATTEMPT TO CAPTURE THE BEAUTY, SCOPE, AND ODDITY OF THE ACTUAL GALACTIC FUNNELS.

APPLAUSE.

THANK YOU. QUESTIONS?

UM. IN THE EXHIBITION CATALOG FOR THE 3527 "FUNNELS AND THE SUBLIME" IT MENTIONS YOU STUDIED UNDER DON DAK. DID HE TEACH YOU HOW TO SEE THE GALACTIC FUNNELS?

NOT AT ALL. I'D SEEN A FEW OF HIS PIECES HERE AND THERE.

I WAS FAMILIAR WITH IT.

BUT PEOPLE HAVE BEEN DOING WORK INSPIRED BY NATURE FOREVER. LANDSCAPE PAINTINGS.   STILL LIFES.

AND PEOPLE HAVE BEEN DOING PAINTINGS OF GEOMETRIC SHAPES FOR OVER A THOUSAND YEARS.

THERE'S JUST NOTHING NEW ABOUT DON DAK'S WORK WHEN YOU VIEW IT IN A, UH, ART HISTORICAL CONTEXT.

THE SIZE OF MY WORK ECHOES THE SCOPE OF THE GALACTIC FUNNELS. AS A RECENT CRITIC SO ELOQUENTLY SAID: "YOU ARE SUCKED INTO THE FUNNEL SHAPE."

APPLAUSE.

I HAVE TIME FOR ONE MORE QUESTION.

154

JASON LUTES

158

159

161

167

TONY MILLIONAIRE

175

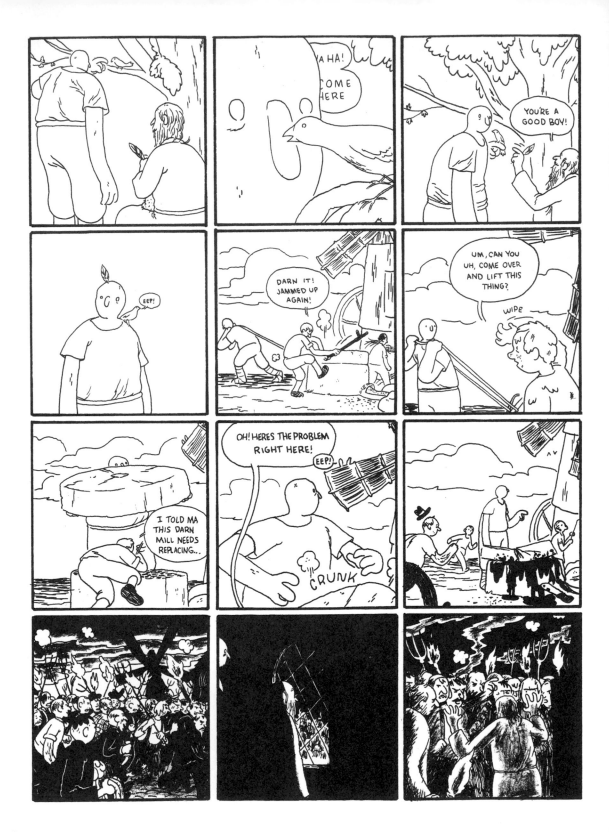

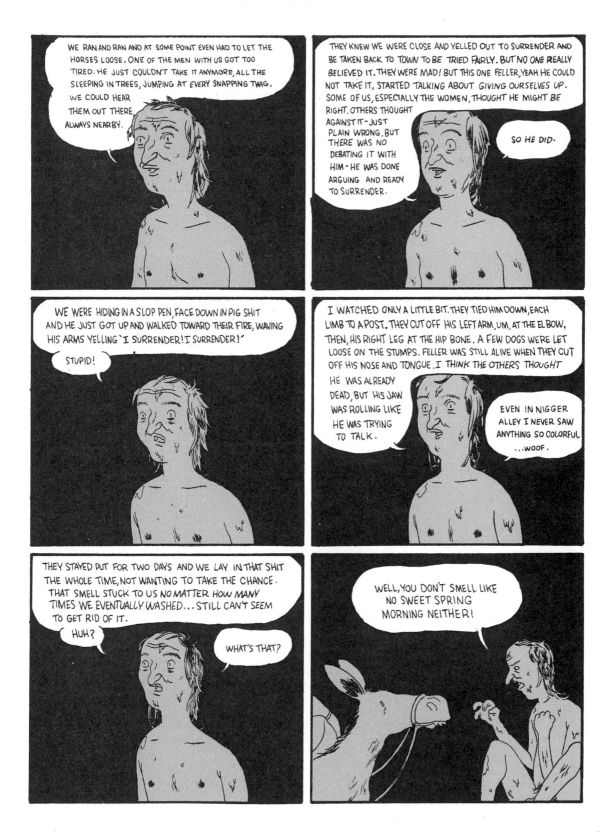

WE RAN AND RAN AND AT SOME POINT EVEN HAD TO LET THE HORSES LOOSE. ONE OF THE MEN WITH US GOT TOO TIRED. HE JUST COULDN'T TAKE IT ANYMORE, ALL THE SLEEPING IN TREES, JUMPING AT EVERY SNAPPING TWIG. WE COULD HEAR THEM OUT THERE, ALWAYS NEARBY.

THEY KNEW WE WERE CLOSE AND YELLED OUT TO SURRENDER AND BE TAKEN BACK TO TOWN TO BE TRIED FAIRLY. BUT NO ONE REALLY BELIEVED IT. THEY WERE MAD! BUT THIS ONE FELLER, YEAH HE COULD NOT TAKE IT, STARTED TALKING ABOUT GIVING OURSELVES UP. SOME OF US, ESPECIALLY THE WOMEN, THOUGHT HE MIGHT BE RIGHT. OTHERS THOUGHT AGAINST IT — JUST PLAIN WRONG. BUT THERE WAS NO DEBATING IT WITH HIM — HE WAS DONE ARGUING AND READY TO SURRENDER.

SO HE DID.

WE WERE HIDING IN A SLOP PEN, FACE DOWN IN PIG SHIT AND HE JUST GOT UP AND WALKED TOWARD THEIR FIRE, WAVING HIS ARMS YELLING 'I SURRENDER! I SURRENDER!'

STUPID!

I WATCHED ONLY A LITTLE BIT. THEY TIED HIM DOWN, EACH LIMB TO A POST. THEY CUT OFF HIS LEFT ARM, UM, AT THE ELBOW, THEN, HIS RIGHT LEG AT THE HIP BONE. A FEW DOGS WERE LET LOOSE ON THE STUMPS. FELLER WAS STILL ALIVE WHEN THEY CUT OFF HIS NOSE AND TONGUE. I THINK THE OTHERS THOUGHT HE WAS ALREADY DEAD, BUT HIS JAW WAS ROLLING LIKE HE WAS TRYING TO TALK.

EVEN IN NIGGER ALLEY I NEVER SAW ANYTHING SO COLORFUL ...WOOF.

THEY STAYED PUT FOR TWO DAYS AND WE LAY IN THAT SHIT THE WHOLE TIME, NOT WANTING TO TAKE THE CHANCE. THAT SMELL STUCK TO US NO MATTER HOW MANY TIMES WE EVENTUALLY WASHED... STILL CAN'T SEEM TO GET RID OF IT.

HUH?

WHAT'S THAT?

WELL, YOU DON'T SMELL LIKE NO SWEET SPRING MORNING NEITHER!

184

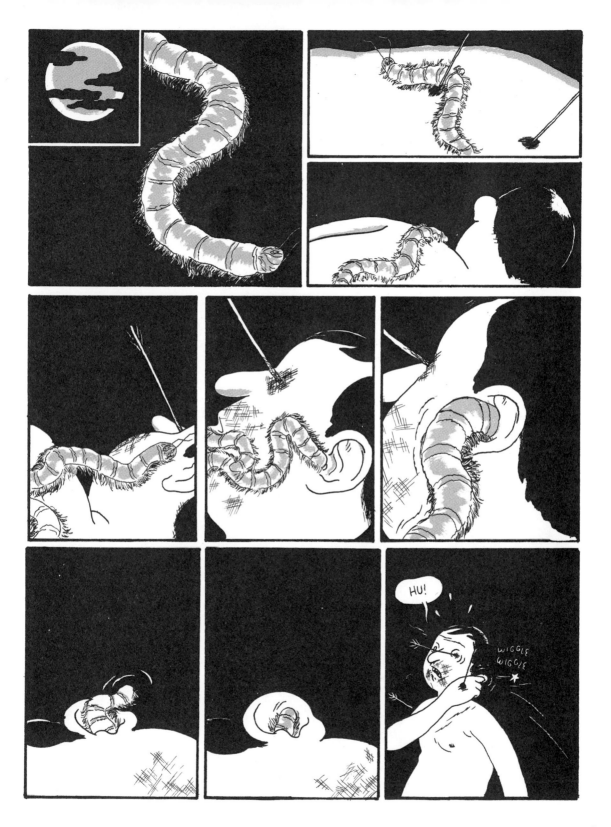

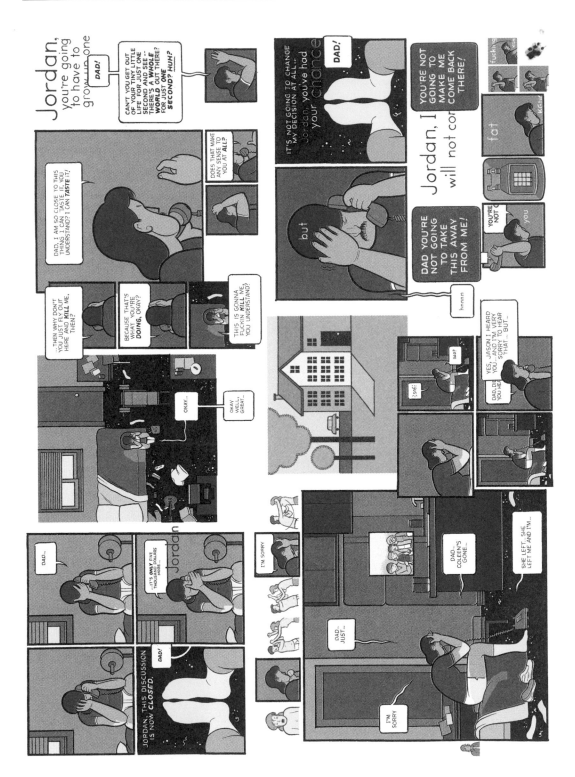

CHRIS WARE

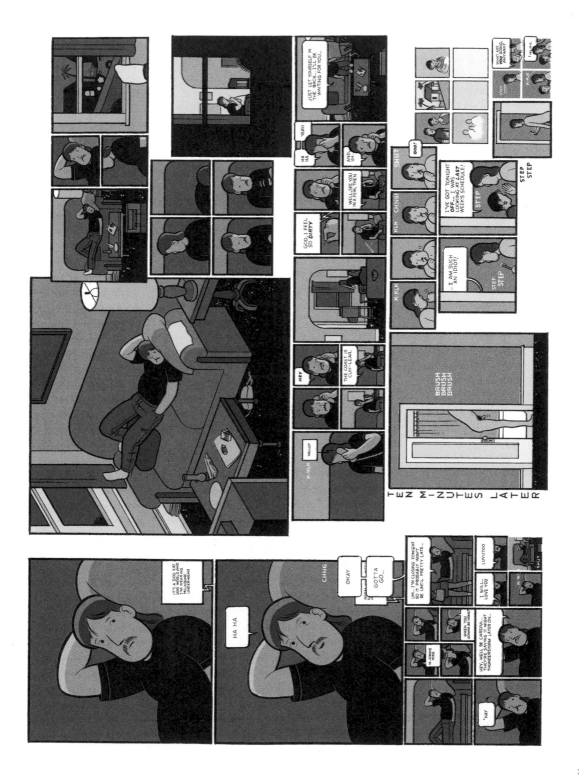

January 1st, 1986.

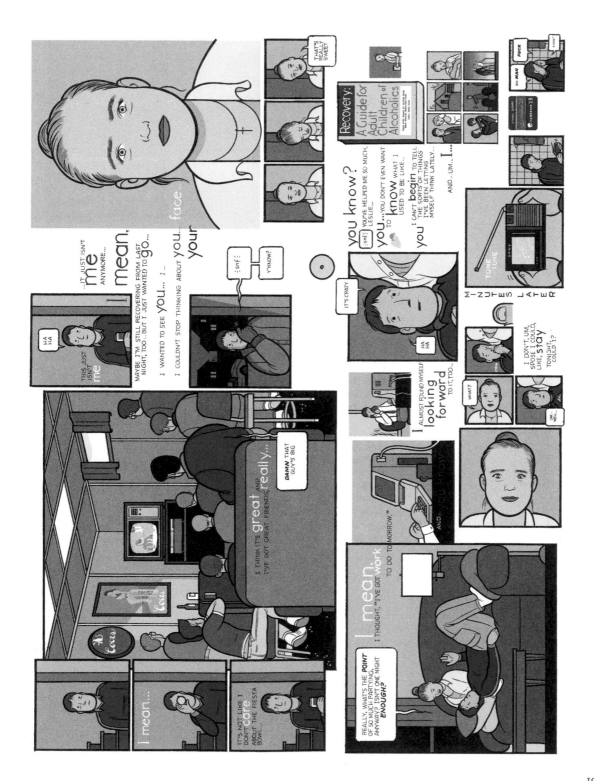

193

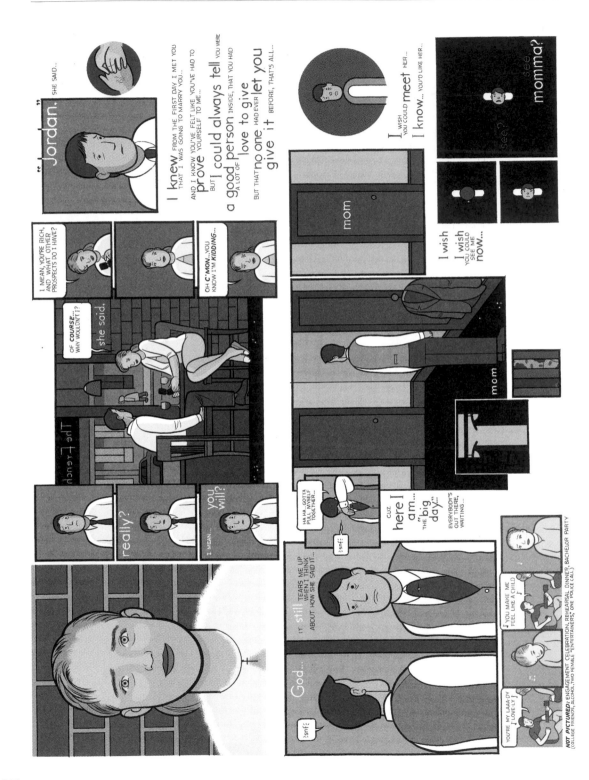

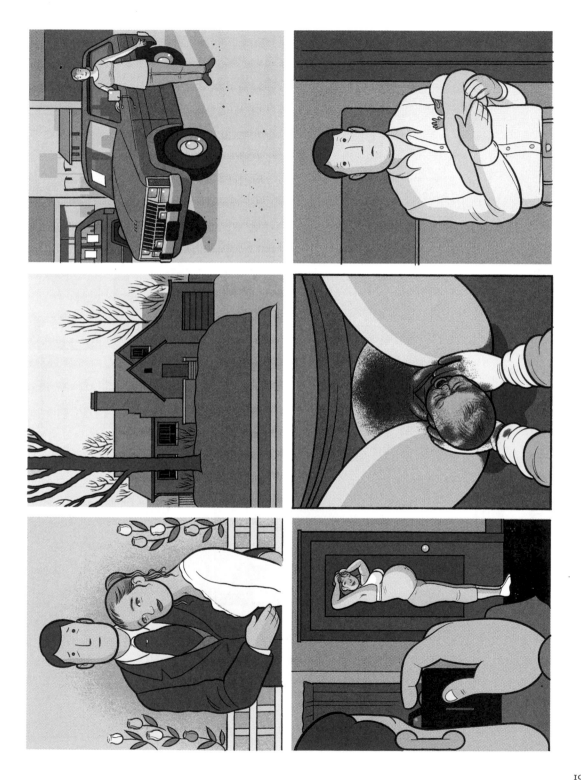

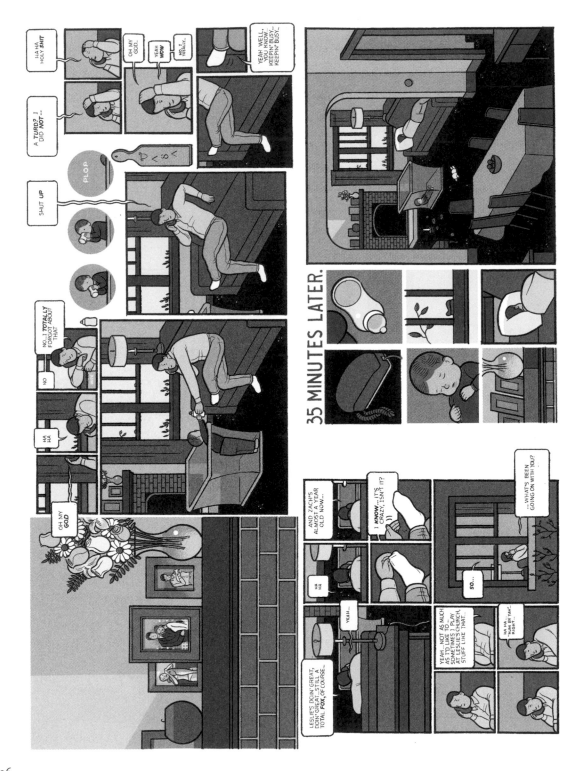

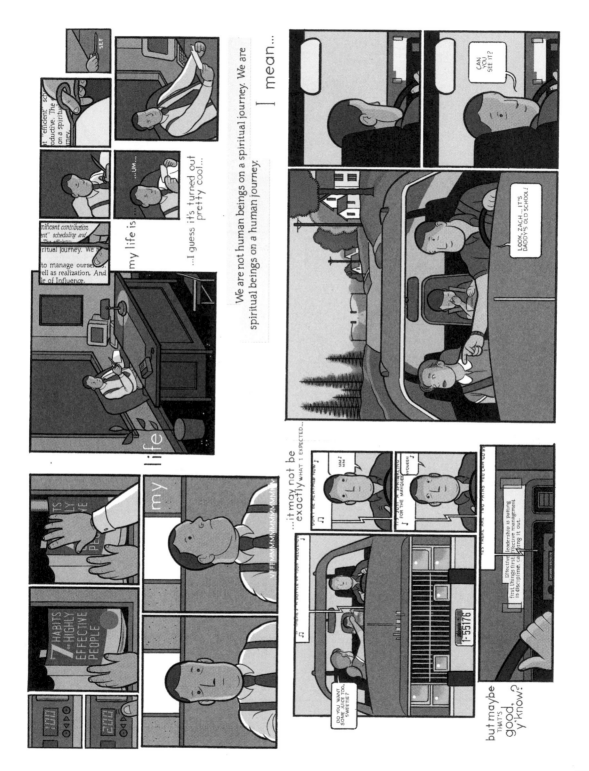

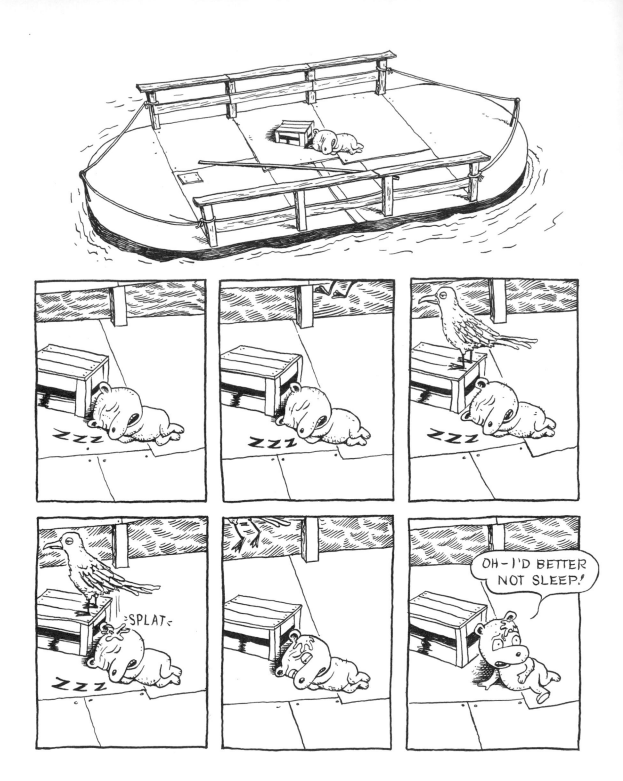

203

205

207

208

216

LAURA PARK

JILLIAN AND MARIKO TAMAKI

Today, everyone in grade ten got pulled into guidance for a talk with Mrs. Hornet.

GUIDANCE

Mrs. Hornet smells like baby powder deodorant. She is a very nervous woman.

INSPIRATION

Mrs. Hornet said she's particularly concerned about people like me, because people like me are prone to depression and depressing stimuli.

Mrs. Hornet says students who are members of the "gothic" culture (i.e. ME) are very fragile.

Truthfully I am always a little depressed but that is just because I am sixteen and everyone is stupid (ha-ha-ha). I doubt it has anything to do with being a goth.

CYCLE OF GRIEF

John Reddear was on the VOLLEYBALL TEAM, not a goth, and he KILLED HIMSELF!!!!

INSPIRATION

How come all the girls on the soccer team aren't in counseling?.

Dear Diary,

Last night Lisa and I tried to
summon the spirit of John Reddear,
but he didn't appear.

Lisa asked what we would do if he did show up.

Nothing, I guess. Ignore him.

I try to go to gym, but am forced to skip class whenever balls are involved. I have this thing about balls. Especially airborne balls. Besides, you can't play golf with one arm. So there I was, thinking and stuff, when Ms. Archer walked up.

Well, well, well. A smoker.

Yesterday during third period I skipped gym and went down to the ravine.

I was just leaving.

Only if you don't have a light on you.

And suddenly I'm talking like there's no tomorrow, which is weird, because I'm not a talker.

It's a rule that if an adult asks to smoke with you, you have to smoke. So we ended up talking and smoking.

I just think it's stupid. I mean, you know, that we're studying all these books... plays... whatever... that everyone studies every year. I mean, they're not even all that interesting, or like, unique. I mean. A LOVE story. No offense.

None taken.

Three things I will not tell Lisa:

1) My heart feels like a piece of chalk stuck in my throat.

2) I feel like I am definitely a witch, although I am technically only starting to be a witch.

3) I have this piece of paper in my bra.

huff!

Last year, all year, Lisa wore a stone shaped like a heart in her bra as a love charm. When she wore her school shirt sometimes it looked like an extra really big nipple. Lisa didn't think so. But I did.

A Wicca charm can be a thing or a spell or an incantation. It doesn't have to be a rock.

My Wicca book says one spell you can do is cut a piece of paper into a strip and write on it, "My heart will bring my love to me." Three times you write that. Then you tape the two ends of the paper together so it makes a loop.

And that's what I'm wearing in my bra now.

236

Uh. Okay. Weirdo. Do you want me to leave or something?

I thought you said you were going to talk to her?

Right. Well, I just decided I was hungry.

I'm a freak.

You're a spaz.

Fuck you.

Lisa took off after school, so I went home and worked on my altar alone. I sprinkled some glitter over my altar and then realized it looked stupid. It took me an hour and two rolls of tape to get it off again.

Ms. Archer and I have this thing now. When we sit for our talks, Ms. Archer holds my cast.

It's just this thing.

She was a painter and a dancer and she was studying to be a writer.

Ms. Archer says she can't stop looking at my eyes.

Before Ms. Archer was a teacher at our school, she used to live in a commune with a bunch of artists.

She says they are very serious.

This morning over breakfast, Mom asked me about suicide. Because of John Reddear, who is now suddenly part of my life.

I said I am not planning on committing suicide.

Apparently I look unwell. Mom says possibly I am losing weight.

Are you coming to lunch?

Oh. No. I have a meeting.

With who?

Ms. Archer is helping me with something.

Right.

flush

Did you finish your card yet? For Katie?

I'm not making Katie Matthews a fucking card.

Sssssshhhh

I don't even know Katie Matthews, let alone give a shit about her fucking dead boyfriend, so fuck it.

SHAKE

Wow.

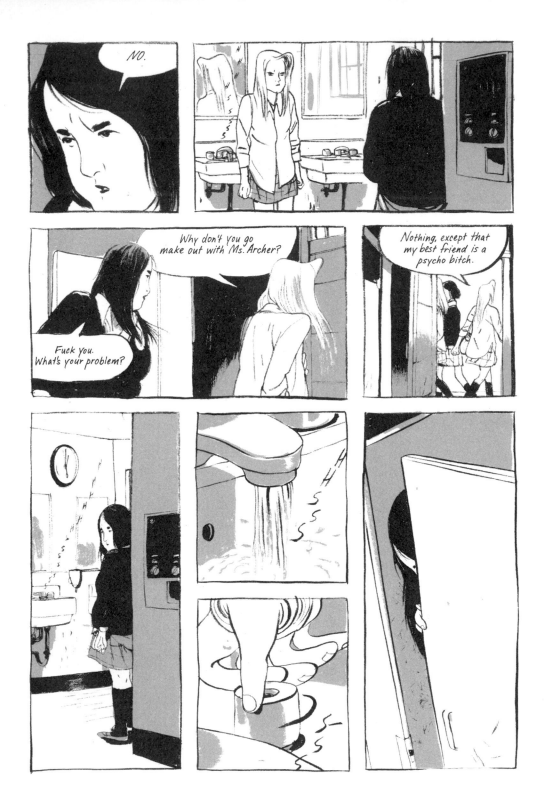

242

Dear Diary,

Books on Wicca are really long and kind of boring.

I think I know what I'm doing, anyway.

My Wicca book says witches take responsibility
for their own actions.

So these are my actions.

They aren't hurting anyone.
So be it.

Lisa is not talking to me.

FINE.

Halloween is not actually a witches' holiday.

The actual Wicca festival is called Samhain Lore, which is at the end of summer.

Samhain Lore is a time to communicate with the dead and feast.

Halloween is when a lot of non-witches dress up like witches.

So it's hard to see people as they really are.

Unless they are dressed up like Barbie or Nixon or Freddy, in which case you know they are lame-o freaks.

Both Lisa and I went as witches. We did not discuss this ahead of time, as we are not speaking.

Did you see that Katie Matthews is back? On Halloween. She's dressed as a ballerina. I had this thought, you know, that she might dress up as a ghost.

244

245

Ms. Archer came as a fortune teller.

Lisa and I went to the park after school to channel the spirits, but it started to rain. So we went home and ate the candy my mom bought for the treaters.

Technically what I said is not a lie.

Technically nothing has happened.

Dear Diary,

For the record, not all Wicca books are boring.
This is what I found in my new book:

The "Charge" comes to each of us in a different
manner. It is that moment in our lives when we
feel the Magick of the Universe coursing through
us for the very first time, and we know beyond
all real and imagined shadows that this calling
to the mysteries is indeed there.

Silver RavenWolf, _To Ride a Silver Broomstick_

DURING MY SENIOR YEAR OF COLLEGE I WAS CULTIVATING AN OVERBLOWN AND UNHEALTHY CRUSH, OR RATHER, AN UBER-CRUSH— THE KIND THAT DOMINATES YOUR MIND TO THE POINT OF COMPLETE PARALYSIS.

FINALLY, AT A RANDOM LOFT PARTY, AND FOLLOWING FOUR SUCCESSIVE BOTTLES OF GUINNESS, I HAD MUSTERED THE COURAGE TO GO UP AND SPEAK TO...

Antoinette

257

I WAS FEELING ODDLY VACANT,
GUIDED BY HER LAST COMMAND—
NOT A THOUGHT IN MY HEAD,
ONLY CEASELESS STATIC.

IT MUST HAVE BEEN THE
WORST HEADACHE OF MY LIFE...

KEVIN HUIZENGA

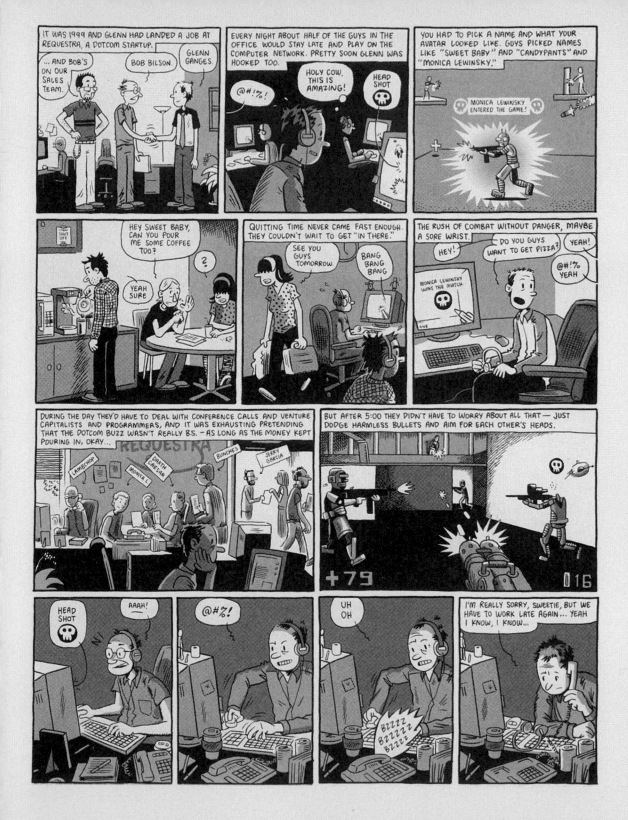

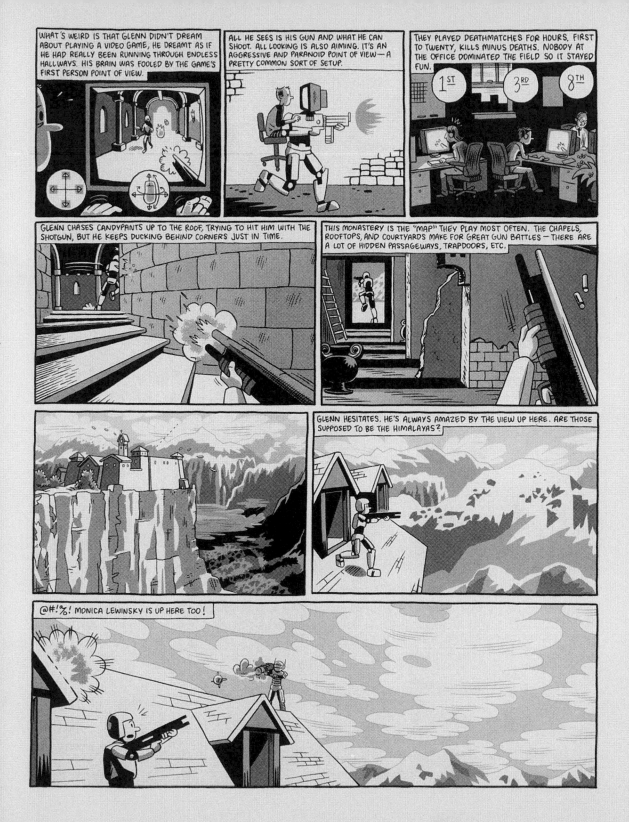

WHAT'S WEIRD IS THAT GLENN DIDN'T DREAM ABOUT PLAYING A VIDEO GAME. HE DREAMT AS IF HE HAD REALLY BEEN RUNNING THROUGH ENDLESS HALLWAYS. HIS BRAIN WAS FOOLED BY THE GAME'S FIRST PERSON POINT OF VIEW.

ALL HE SEES IS HIS GUN AND WHAT HE CAN SHOOT. ALL LOOKING IS ALSO AIMING. IT'S AN AGGRESSIVE AND PARANOID POINT OF VIEW — A PRETTY COMMON SORT OF SETUP.

THEY PLAYED DEATHMATCHES FOR HOURS. FIRST TO TWENTY, KILLS MINUS DEATHS. NOBODY AT THE OFFICE DOMINATED THE FIELD SO IT STAYED FUN.

1ST   3RD   8TH

GLENN CHASES CANDYPANTS UP TO THE ROOF, TRYING TO HIT HIM WITH THE SHOTGUN, BUT HE KEEPS DUCKING BEHIND CORNERS JUST IN TIME.

THIS MONASTERY IS THE "MAP" THEY PLAY MOST OFTEN. THE CHAPELS, ROOFTOPS, AND COURTYARDS MAKE FOR GREAT GUN BATTLES — THERE ARE A LOT OF HIDDEN PASSAGEWAYS, TRAPDOORS, ETC.

GLENN HESITATES. HE'S ALWAYS AMAZED BY THE VIEW UP HERE. ARE THOSE SUPPOSED TO BE THE HIMALAYAS?

@#!%! MONICA LEWINSKY IS UP HERE TOO!

263

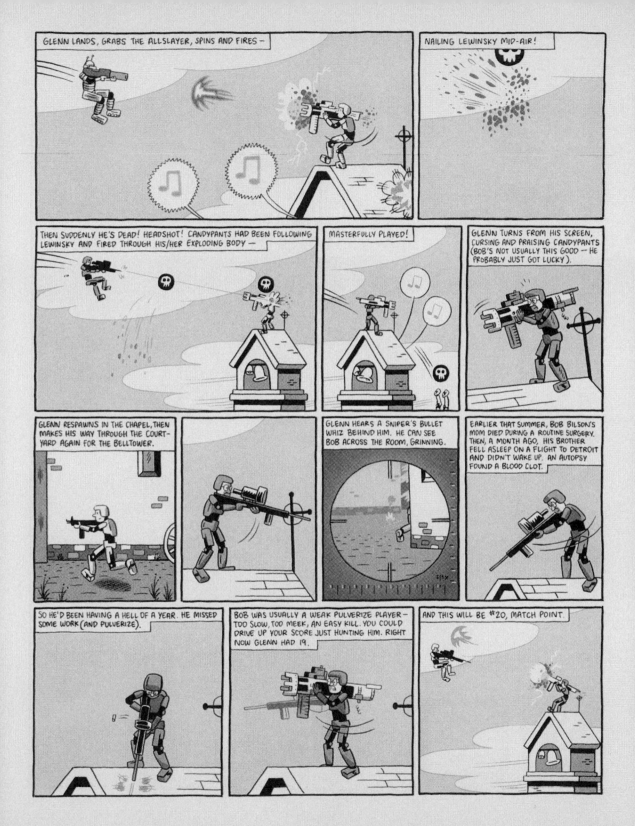

GLENN LANDS, GRABS THE ALLSLAYER, SPINS AND FIRES —

NAILING LEWINSKY MID-AIR!

THEN SUDDENLY HE'S DEAD! HEADSHOT! CANDYPANTS HAD BEEN FOLLOWING LEWINSKY AND FIRED THROUGH HIS/HER EXPLODING BODY —

MASTERFULLY PLAYED!

GLENN TURNS FROM HIS SCREEN, CURSING AND PRAISING CANDYPANTS (BOB'S NOT USUALLY THIS GOOD — HE PROBABLY JUST GOT LUCKY).

GLENN RESPAWNS IN THE CHAPEL, THEN MAKES HIS WAY THROUGH THE COURT-YARD AGAIN FOR THE BELLTOWER.

GLENN HEARS A SNIPER'S BULLET WHIZ BEHIND HIM. HE CAN SEE BOB ACROSS THE ROOM, GRINNING.

EARLIER THAT SUMMER, BOB BILSON'S MOM DIED DURING A ROUTINE SURGERY. THEN, A MONTH AGO, HIS BROTHER FELL ASLEEP ON A FLIGHT TO DETROIT AND DIDN'T WAKE UP. AN AUTOPSY FOUND A BLOOD CLOT.

SO HE'D BEEN HAVING A HELL OF A YEAR. HE MISSED SOME WORK (AND PULVERIZE).

BOB WAS USUALLY A WEAK PULVERIZE PLAYER — TOO SLOW, TOO MEEK, AN EASY KILL. YOU COULD DRIVE UP YOUR SCORE JUST HUNTING HIM. RIGHT NOW GLENN HAD 19.

AND THIS WILL BE #20, MATCH POINT.

BUT THEN ONE EVENING GLENN REALIZED:

IT'S SPACEWAR!

HEY, DO YOU WANT TO COME OVER TO MY HOUSE? WE JUST GOT A COMPUTER

COOL

IN 1962 A STUDENT AT M.I.T. WROTE THE FIRST COMPUTER GAME—"SPACEWAR." IT WAS INCLUDED WITH EARLY PCS FOR MANY YEARS.

256k "HARD DRIVE"

YES!

BEEP

ONE MORE?

TWO PLAYERS CONTROL "SPACESHIPS" AND DUEL ON A BLACK SCREEN DOTTED WITH A FEW WHITE PIXELS.

(A DIFFERENT M.I.T. STUDENT WROTE A PROGRAM THAT WOULD COORDINATE THESE "STARS" WITH THE ACTUAL NIGHT SKY.)

PLAYERS FIRE "TORPEDOS," TRYING TO DAMAGE THE OTHER'S "SHIELD."

PLAYER 1   PLAYER 2
S   S

MANY YEARS LATER, MUCH MORE CODE GOES INTO WRITING PULVERIZE, BUT ESSENTIALLY IT'S THE SAME THING— ABSTRACT COMBAT.

...AND WHEN I REALIZED THAT, I GUESS IT DIDN'T SEEM SO WRONG TO ENJOY IT AS MUCH AS I DID...

UNDERNEATH, IT'S JUST DOTS SHOOTING DOTS AT DOTS...

I DON'T KNOW... WHAT ABOUT THOSE KIDS WHO SHOT UP THEIR SCHOOL? MASSACRED THEIR CLASSMATES?

WEREN'T THEY INSPIRED BY THAT GAME?

NO...

YEAH, BUT...

IT'S SO DIFFERENT...

"INSPIRED." I DON'T KNOW... I MEAN...

WHEN SOMEONE "DIES" IN THE GAME, THEY COME RIGHT BACK. THAT'S DIFFERENT THAN REAL DYING.

OR REAL KILLING!

AND IT'S DIFFERENT WHEN YOU PLAY WITH OTHER GUYS AND YOU'RE ALL HAVING A GOOD TIME TOGETHER...

THE LAST THING YOU WANT TO DO IS REALLY... YOU KNOW... ACTUALLY SHOOT AND KILL SOMEONE!! YOU JUST WANT TO PLAY MORE!

NOT, YOU KNOW...

WELL, YOU GUYS SHOULDN'T BE @#!%ING AROUND WHEN REQUESTRA'S NOT DOING SO WELL!

I KNOW...

...AND I STILL THINK IT'S A @#!%ED UP WAY TO SPEND YOUR TIME.

YEAH...

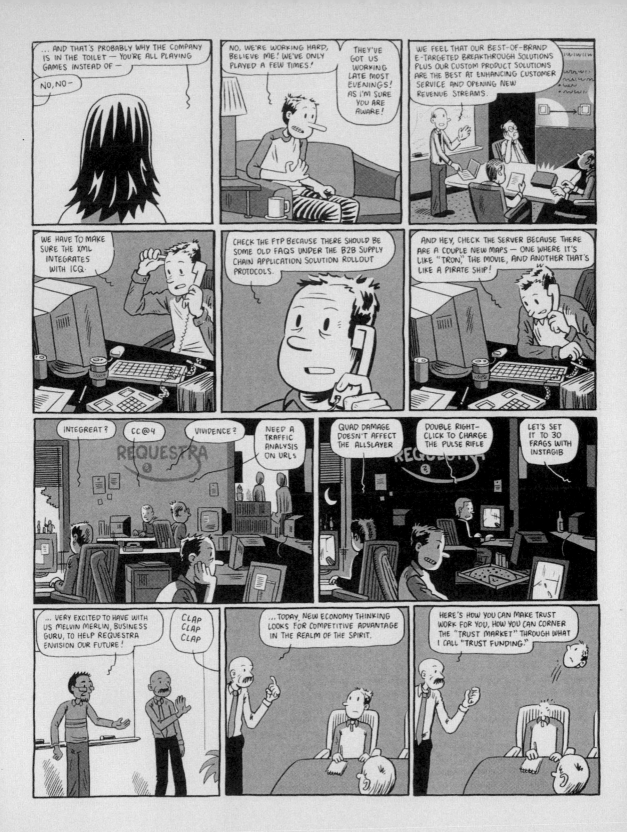

ONE OF THEIR FAVORITES WAS A TROPICAL ISLAND MAP NAMED "REEFLEX" AND THEY VISIT IT AGAIN TONIGHT. THE WAVES LAPPING, GULLS CALLING OVER THE GUNFIRE. GLENN FIGHTS HIS WAY FROM THE BEACH THROUGH THE THICK, SHADOWY JUNGLE TO ONE OF THE CAVES,

WHICH LEADS TO ONE OF THE THREE ROCKY PEAKS, WHERE HE HAS A BREATHTAKING VIEW OF THE WHOLE COMPLEX, GOOD FOR SNIPING.

ANOTHER WAS "ORBITUS," A SPACE STATION HOVERING ABOVE A RED PLANET.

AS HE LEAPS FROM PLATFORM TO PLATFORM IN THE LOW GRAVITY, GLENN FEELS A DIZZY FEELING IN HIS GUT, AND LOOKING/AIMING DOWN AT THE PLANET BELOW, HE CAN SEE THE GLOW OF VOLCANIC ERUPTIONS.

"FOG OF WAR" HAD BEEN A FAVORITE FOR A FEW WEEKS. ARMED WITH ONLY SNIPER RIFLES AND CHAINSAWS, THEY WANDER A VAST SCORCHED PLAIN, SEARCHING THE HORIZON FOR EACH OTHER AND HIDING IN THE DRIFTING BANKS OF FOG.

POW

AND NEXT WE HAVE "HALLWAYS TO HELL," WHICH IS SELF-EXPLANATORY...

ANOTHER FAVORITE MAP WAS BASED ON AN OFFICE, WITH CUBICLES AND FAX MACHINES AND A BREAK ROOM AND EVERYTHING,

ONLY THE PLAYERS ARE SHRUNK TO THE SIZE OF MICE. THE CUBICLES ARE LIKE CANYONS, AND OF COURSE PULVERIZE IS ON EVERY SCREEN...

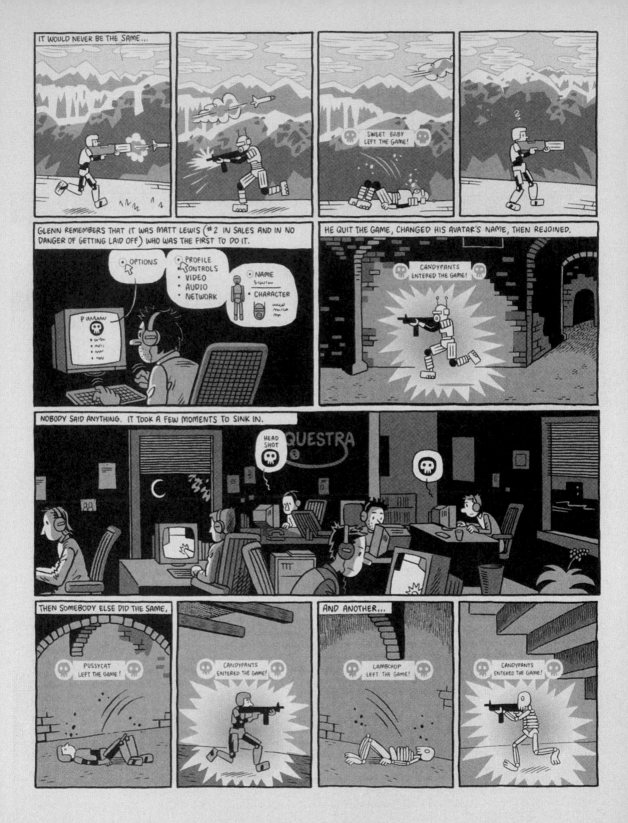

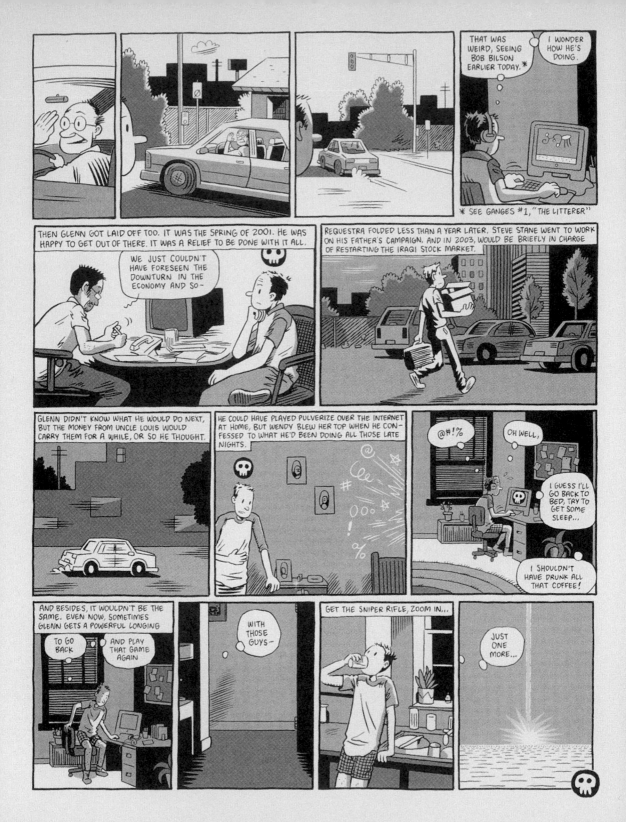

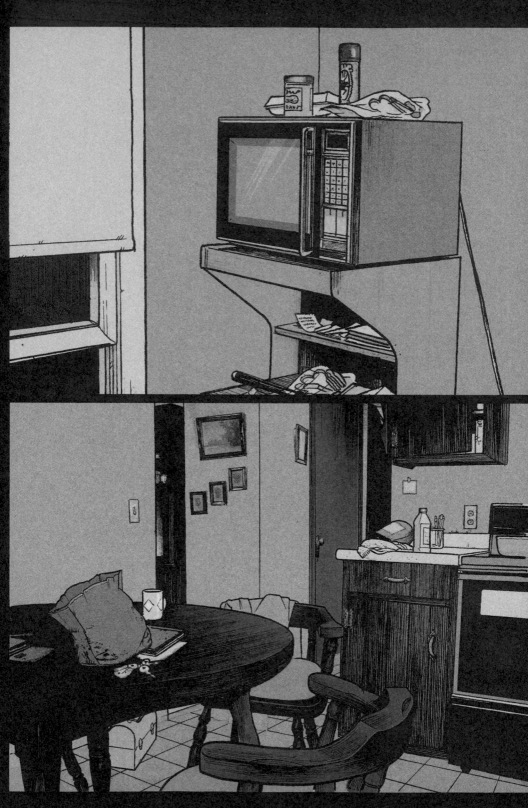

GILBERT HERNANDEZ

15

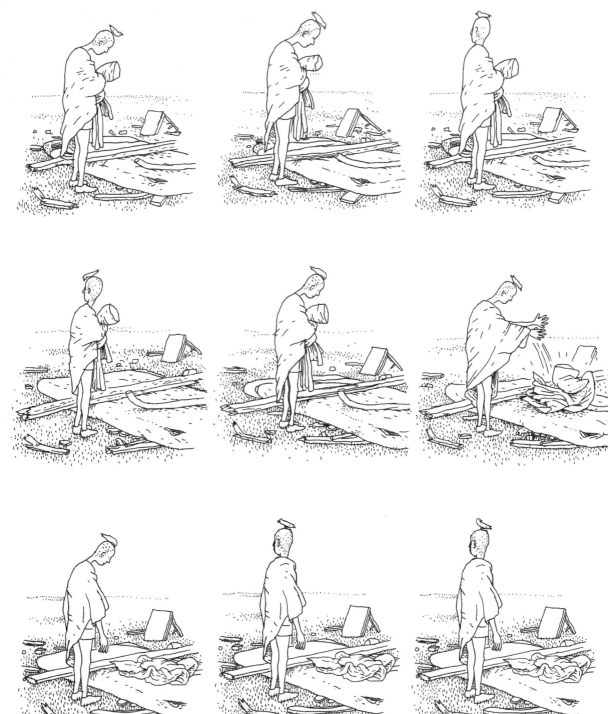

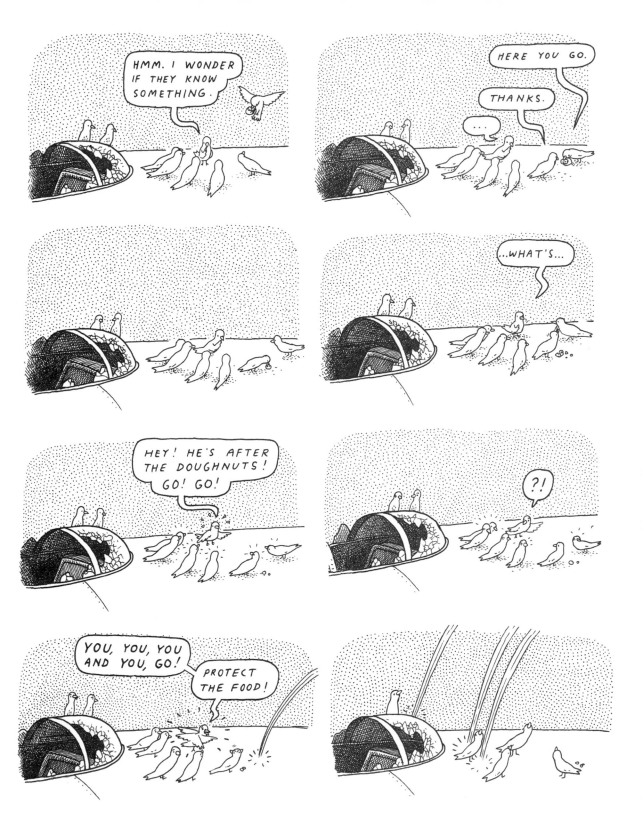

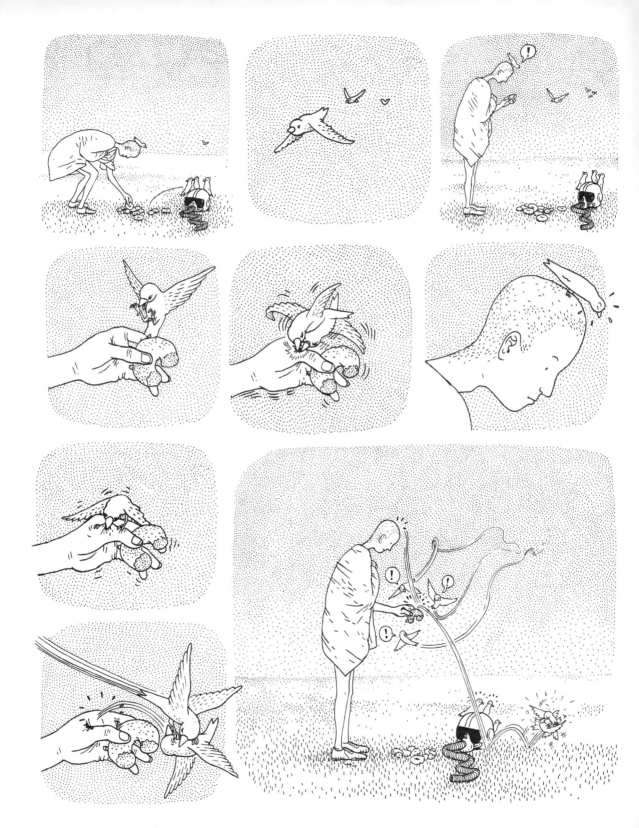

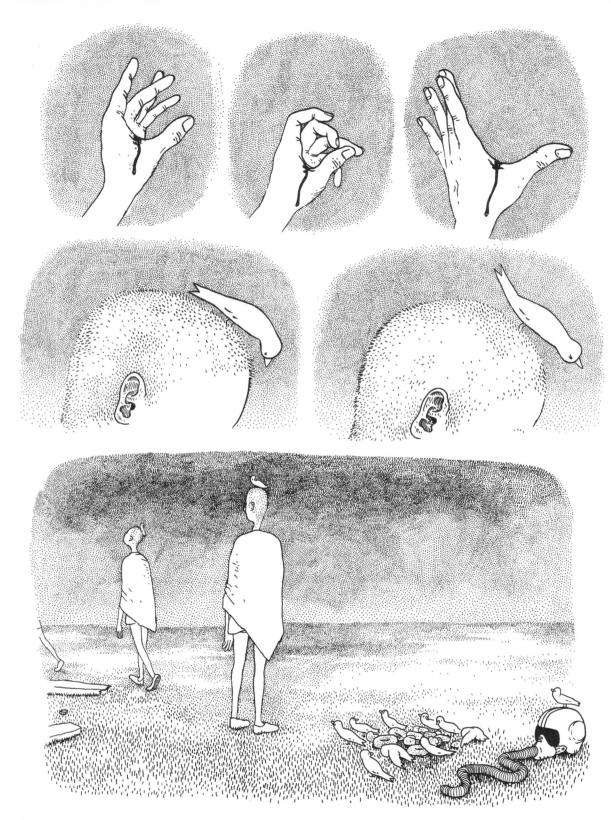

Contributors' Notes

Doug Allen is probably best known for his long-running underground strip, *Steven,* which appeared in a number of alternative papers around the United States and has been collected into several volumes published by Kitchen Sink Press and Fantagraphics. He also worked as an illustrator and played bass in the new-wave country band Rubber Rodeo in the '80s. He and bandmate Gary Leib collaborated on a series of gallery murals and a magazine called *Idiotland,* and he worked on several movie projects, including the SpongeBob movie and *American Splendor.* Allen currently lives with his wife and two children in Rockland County, New York.

■ In this "politically correct" era, it is sometimes a challenge to find a way of poking fun at people without offending anyone, but over the years I find I am constantly drawn to one particular subspecies of human, the ever amusing "hillbilly." Don't get me wrong, I've spent thirty years playing in various old-time, bluegrass, and hillbilly-style bands, worshiping a very stereotyped illusion that may never have really existed, but fascinated me in all its rural barnyard bliss, and that the last few generations have distilled into the toothless, inbred, road-kill eating abomination that Jed Clampett and his family brought into our living rooms during the '60s. Being born in Greenwich, Connecticut, I have no right to pretend I know anything about the real people who proudly call themselves hillbillies, but it sure is a rich source of imagery for drawing dirty comics. Yee-HAH!

Peter Bagge is best known as the creator of the '90s alternative comics series *Hate,* featuring the misadventures of the semi-autobiographical Buddy Bradley. He also wrote and/or illustrated several other comic series, such as *Neat Stuff, Apocalypse Nerd, Yeah!,* and *Sweatshop,* and is a past and present contributor to *Reason, Mad, Weekly World News, Screw,* and many other publications, as well as the managing editor of R. Crumb's *Weirdo Magazine* in the '80s.

A New York native, Bagge is a longtime resident of Seattle, Washington.

■ This story was part of a series called "Founding Fathers Funnies" that appeared as short backup stories in a miniseries I recently completed called *Apocalypse Nerd.* The purpose of the series was not only to share my fascination with the Founders but also to show what amusingly flawed people they could be.

Unlike the other well-known Founders, Paul Revere wasn't a man of letters. He was a middle-class craftsman who spent little or no time second-guessing himself or fine-tuning his philosophy. Still, he was very clear-cut in his beliefs, and those beliefs were reflected in everything he did, including his approach to his own artistic creations. His attitude surely clashed with that of his friend and neighbor John Copley, who had the more typically vain and self-glorious personality that usually comes with being an artist, and this strip is a speculation of what that clash might have sounded like.

Gabrielle Bell is the author of *Cecil and Jordan in New York* and the Ignatz award-winning semi-autobiographical series *Lucky.* She has contributed to several anthologies including *Mome* and *Kramers Ergot.* She lives in Brooklyn, New York, and continues to draw comics.

▪ This story was originally written for the *New York Times* Op-ed Summerscapes page, but it turned out to be too long and possibly too dark. To me, it was an achievement that I couldn't at the time exactly define, so I did the story for myself and included it in my comic book *Lucky*. It's a story about a girl's naive attempt to escape her circumstances and live a better life on her own, only to find out she can't because she is too young. In her failure she sees her life more clearly and consequently moves a little closer toward the life she wants. Since then I've recognized it as a theme in my life and my work: the attempt to escape, the realization that there is no escape, and (perhaps, hopefully) some maturity in coping.

Matt Broersma grew up in South Texas, surrounded by steers, oil fields, and cowboy karaoke bars. After spells as a singing bartender in Osaka and a reporter in San Francisco, he took up drawing, setting many of his comic books in the American West. His longer stories, from publishers including Bayard Jeunesse, Drawn & Quarterly, Éditions Flblb, Fantagraphics, and Vertige Graphic, range from thrillers and Westerns to sketchbook travelogues and autobiography. He has also contributed to a number of anthologies, including *42,000km*, *Black*, *Comix2000*, *L'Eprouvette*, *Polyominos*, *Spoutnik*, and *Top Shelf*.

▪ I have always found the frontier fascinating and mysterious. I grew up surrounded by relics of the Old West—pioneer cabins, Indian reservations, abandoned silver-mining towns, and the like—and always wanted to use something of that atmosphere in a story. In this comic I looked at the West through the lens of the familiar modern world. The idea was to gradually scrape away the layers of familiarity until the strange and mythical landscape of the past was revealed.

Daniel Clowes was born in Chicago in 1961. He studied art at the Pratt Institute in Brooklyn, New York, though he considers himself to be largely self-taught. Fantagraphics Books began publishing his first comic book series, *Lloyd Llewellyn*, in 1985. He produced six issues, borrowing heavily from such popular genres as science fiction/horror films of the '50s, superheroes, and detective novels. As *Lloyd Llewellyn* progressed, Clowes's artwork developed, suggesting the stark, atmospheric work of '50s EC crime and science fiction artists like Johnny Craig and Bernie Krigstein. It was this progression that set the stage for Clowes's new Fantagraphics title, *Eightball*.

Eightball's evolution and increasing maturity has been remarkable. From the early, surreal *Like a Velvet Glove Cast in Iron* to his savage take on the comics industry in *Pussey!* to Clowes's breakthrough hit, *Ghost World*, and his most recent opus, *David Boring*, which features some of the most intricate plotting and layered thematic writing in comics, *Eightball* has earned the artist a large following (and has spawned eight graphic novel collections). Clowes has amassed multiple Harvey, Eisner, and Ignatz Comics Awards through the years, in all the major categories.

In 2001, MGM/UA released the *Ghost World* motion picture. Directed by Terry Zwigoff, the man responsible for the critical and commercial documentary success *Crumb*, from a screenplay by Clowes and Zwigoff, the film was one of the top five most critically acclaimed films of the year, and received numerous film awards and nominations, including Academy Award and Golden Globe nominations for Clowes and Zwigoff for "Best Adapted Screenplay." Clowes's second screenplay, *Art School Confidential* was released as a film in 2006.

His comics have appeared in *Details*, *The New Yorker*, *Blab!*, *Cracked*, *World Art*, and the *Village Voice*, to name but a few. Clowes has drawn album covers for numerous bands and done illustration work for SubPop Records and the infamous OK Soda from Coca-Cola. Clowes did the animation for the Ramones video "I Don't Wanna Grow Up," and the movie poster for Todd Solandz's acclaimed film *Happiness*. *Ghost World* is the best-selling book in Fantagraphics' twenty-five-plus-year history with over 100,000 copies in print. The twenty-second issue of *Eightball* was released in early 2002, marking the first full-color, stand-alone issue of the series in its twelve year history. Clowes's *David Boring* was published by Pantheon Books in 2000 to great critical and commercial acclaim, including raves from *TIME*, the *New York Times Book Review*, *The New Yorker*, and many others, and his most recent book, *Twentieth Century Eightball*, was released in 2002 to equal acclaim. Currently Clowes lives in Oakland, California, with his wife, Erika.

- "Justin M. Damiano" was written for the collection *The Book of Other People*, in which the editor, the novelist Zadie Smith, invited twenty-two other authors to create and write a story about an invented character.

Al Columbia (b. 1970) currently lives in Connecticut with his partner, Kathleen, their eight-year-old daughter, Miranda Rose, and a hyperactive and mischievous white cat named Newspaper.

- "5:45 A.M." is an idea, or moment, that developed from panel to panel without a script or goal in mind. My experience in creating the story was not unlike the experience of reading it. I moved from room to room, not knowing what I would find next. The cause of the widow's death remains a mystery to this date, even to me.

Robert Dennis Crumb (born August 30, 1943), often credited simply as R. Crumb, is an American artist and illustrator recognized for the distinctive style of his drawings and his critical, satirical, subversive view of the American mainstream. He currently lives in Southern France.

Crumb was a founder of the underground comix movement and is regarded as its most prominent figure. Though one of the most celebrated of comic book artists, Crumb's entire career has unfolded outside the mainstream comic book publishing industry. One of his most recognized works is the *Keep on Truckin'* comic, which became a widely distributed fixture of pop culture in the '70s. Others are the characters Devil Girl, Fritz the Cat, and Mr. Natural. He also illustrated the album covers for *Cheap Thrills* by Big Brother and the Holding Company and the compilation album *The Music Never Stopped: Roots of the Grateful Dead*.

CF b. 1979

- I drew this during winter in Liberty, Maine. I was in an apartment connected to a tool museum. Every day I would put off making a meal for myself and every day my friend Annie would surprise me by making something nice. I had just finished making a crystal radio before I left Providence, and I would listen to it when I was drawing sometimes. Dan and Amy would come home at night and we would have dinner. It was a good situation for me, lucky.

I'm generally bad at getting back to people, but you may write to P.O. Box 913, Providence RI 02901 or (!!) wizardacorn@hotmail.

Sammy Harkham (b. 1980) lives in Los Angeles. He edits the comics anthology *Kramers Ergot*, and has had comics published in *Vice*, *Drawn & Quarterly Showcase*, and *Arthur*. His book *Poor Sailor* was published in 2005 by Ginkgo Press. He is currently working on his ongoing comic book series, *Crickets*.

- I start each strip with a handful of ideas and let things develop and change on the page. With the second chapter of "Black Death," I had a couple things I wanted to expand on from chapter one, but went into it pretty blindly, letting the characters and situations direct the tone and unfolding of the strip.

Tim Hensley was born in Bloomington, Indiana, in 1966, but now lives in Hollywood with his wife. He is currently completing a comic story called "Gropius" being serialized in the Fantagraphics publication *Mome*; the strips included here are an excerpt.

- If you read any teenager comic ever drawn, such as *Debbi*, *Binky*, or *Freddy*, there is usually an argument between a temperamental father and his daughter, often over a boy. The last page of "The Argument" was very difficult to draw. I knew that an unlikely sexual position would be an opportunity for an extremely morbid sight gag, so I went to the "sexuality" section at Borders hoping to find something along the lines of a *Complete Idiot's Guide to the Kama Sutra* for photo reference. When I arrived there, I found a couple browsing in that section. I felt I might embarrass them and myself to lean past to flip through a book of couplings next to them. I thus retreated to pretend to scan spines in the Graphic Novels section. When I returned, there was an older woman by herself; I didn't interrupt her. Eventually I was able to choose a book unaccompanied, but then I had to purchase it downstairs. I placed the book face-down with the bar code up, but the person behind the register turned it over; she said not a thing, but looked amused. I eventually chose a position that the book said was to compensate for a man's lack of endowment lengthwise.

Gilbert Hernandez is the co-creator of *Love and Rockets* and was born with a comic book in his hand. Growing up reading just about every kind of comic book there was in the '60s and '70s, he developed such an appreciation for the medium that it led him to believe comics could be a place for personal expression. The only type of comics that he didn't read were romance comics, and he has ironically been considered mostly a writer of, well, girly comics.

- I serialized a graphic novel called *Julio's Day* in *Love and Rockets* about a man's one hundred year life. It was supposed to be one hundred pages long, but when it fell short of that, I decided to add two more chapters to be included in the collection later. One character that didn't have much going on in the story was Julio's dad, so I put him in "Papa" as a chapter to be included early in the complete book.

Kevin Huizenga was born near Chicago and now lives near St. Louis. More info about his books and self-published zines can be found at usscatastrophe.com.

Ben Katchor's monthly strip on the subjects of architecture and urban design appears in *Metropolis* magazine. He has collaborated with musician Mark Mulcahy on two musical theater productions — *The Slug Bearers of Kayrol Island* and *The Rosenbach Company* — and is working on a third, *A Checkroom Romance*, scheduled to premiere in 2009. He is an associate professor at Parsons The New School, in New York City, where he teaches visual narrative. For more information please visit www.katchor.com.

- In these strips, I've tried to channel my violent revolutionary impulses into a form that does not result in my arrest. I derive my inspiration from the collapse of capitalism. Gravel driveways, testicular nationalism, and antibacterialism are all byproducts of that system. The unemployed bankers and stockbrokers of America should be subject to compulsory reeducation in picture-story writing! Boycott "pure" prose fiction and expose the fallacy of "mental images"!

Kaz was born in Hoboken, New Jersey, and now lives in Hollywood, California, with his wife, Linda Marotta. Kaz won an Emmy last year for his work writing on Cartoon Network's *Camp Lazlo* show. He's been busy writing and drawing on various film and TV projects and is currently a storyboard writer and director on the crew of Disney's *Phineas and Ferb* cartoon show. Somehow he manages to get his comic strip, *Underworld*, out every week.

- The comic strips in this edition were done under duress and much personal pain and suffering. They are a cry for help from a poor devil who's got no hope of ever finding peace in his lifetime.

Since 1971, **Aline Kominsky-Crumb** has been one of the seminal figures in American comics. She was one of the first contributors to the groundbreaking *Wommen's Comix*, and, with Diane Noomin, founded the underground classic comic *Twisted Sisters* in 1976. She was one of the first artists to do autobiographical comics and develop the graphic novel form.

Kominsky-Crumb has also been a longtime collaborator with her husband, the famed cartoonist Robert Crumb, on such comic classics as *Dirty Laundry Comics; Weirdo* magazine, where

Ms. Crumb was also an editor; *Self Loathing Comics;* and their joint work for several years for *The New Yorker.*

Michael Kupperman lives and works in Brooklyn, where he has been voted "most improved" three years running. His comics and illustrations have appeared in publications ranging from *The New Yorker* to *Screw.* His book of comics, *Snake 'N' Bacon's Cartoon Cabaret,* appeared in 2000 (good timing), and has recently been translated into French by La Cinquieme Couche (the title is the same). Also, an animated Snake 'N' Bacon pilot with live-action segments was recently completed for Cartoon Network's *Adult Swim,* and they're "definitely" going to broadcast it sometime this year. Currently Michael's comics appear in *Tales Designed to Thrizzle,* published by Fantagraphics.

■ Mark Twain looked up from the typewriter, his brow furrowed. "I'm stuck!" he complained. "I'm trying to write a statement for Michael Kupperman about why he's turned us into a comics sensation, for this big egghead book."

"Just tell them we're awesome," replied Albert Einstein. Just then an object came smashing through the window—a brick with a message tied to it!

Twain read it. "The Pope has been kidnapped!" he announced, and then the two great men leapt into action and rescued the Pope (who was very grateful). "Only we could have an adventure like this within a statement of artistic purpose," pointed out Einstein.

Jason Lutes has been writing and drawing comics since he could pick up a crayon, and has been getting paid for it since 1991, when his first mini-comics were sold on consignment through record and comics shops in Providence, Rhode Island, and San Francisco, California. After graduating from the Rhode Island School of Design, he worked day jobs as a dishwasher, production assistant, and art director before making the leap to full-time cartoonist. Aside from *Jar of Fools,* his first comics novel, and *Berlin* (excerpted herein), he drew *The Fall* (written by Ed Brubaker), and wrote *Houdini: The Handcuff King* (drawn by Nick Bertozzi). He now lives in rural Vermont with his partner and daughter, and teaches part time at the Center for Cartoon Studies while working to complete the last volume of his *Berlin* trilogy.

■ I have been working on *Berlin* for thirteen years now, and my feelings about the project have gone through every imaginable permutation. I had originally planned to complete all three books by the time I turned forty, but my fortieth birthday passed in 2007 with the second volume still unfinished. *Berlin: City of Smoke* was finally published in the fall of 2008, and with that milestone I resolved to complete the final volume within four years. Over the years I have grown deeply attached to the characters that inhabit Berlin and am thoroughly invested in following their various trajectories to whatever specific ends await them, but my greatest frustration as a cartoonist is having so many other stories that I want to tell. Such is the nature of this time-consuming medium—or at least the nature my exceedingly slow work habits. I try to reconcile these feelings by exploring the story at hand in as much depth and with as much attention as I can muster.

Tony Millionaire grew up in Gloucester, Massachusetts, and attended the Massachusetts College of Art. He is the creator of the syndicated comic strip, *Maakies,* which has been collected by Fantagraphics, who also published his graphic novel, *Billy Hazelnuts.* He creates the ongoing adventures of Sock Monkey, published by Dark Horse Comics. His comic strip *Maakies* has been adapted to the small screen as *The Drinky Crow Show* for Cartoon Network's *Adult Swim.* He now lives in Pasadena, California. More information can be found at www.maakies.com.

■ In 1994 I was trying to think of a name for my new strip about Drinky Crow. I didn't want to call it "Drinky Crow" because I wasn't sure how much drinking would end up in there. My friend Spike Vrusho saw a tugboat in New York harbor with a big *M* on the smokestack, and he screeched "MAAAAAKIES!" That's why you'll find a tiny tugboat in every strip.

Jerry Moriarty: Old, lazy guy possessed of ART guilt. Published sporadically as an illustrator, cartoonist, and painter for fifty years since art school. A self-described PAINTOONIST (TOON likes story-telling, PAINT does not), he is able to avoid the responsibility of a profession.

- SALLY is a twelve-year-old girl from 1950. She is the artist-me and much smarter than the everyday-me. She is discovering puberty on her own in 1950, that was before Barbie, Britney, or *Playboy*. Now she is fourteen and known to me as SALLY PINBOY. It is all a trip in. Isn't it? Or not . . .

Anders Nilsen is the author and artist of several graphic novels and comics, including *Big Questions, The End,* and *Monologues for the Coming Plague,* as well as the Ignatz Award–winning *Don't Go Where I Can't Follow* and *Dogs and Water.* He currently lives with his wife and cat in Chicago.

- My hand still hurts from drawing all those dots.

Gary Panter is a painter, cartoonist, puppet-maker, lightshow artist, and musician. He earned a degree in painting from East Texas State University in 1974.

His cartoon drawings, emerging out of the punk rock movement of the late '70s, were recently featured in a three-city museum show, Masters of Comic Art, honoring fifteen comic artists of the twentieth century. He is known for his comic character Jimbo, and also for innovative illustration work, having done album covers for Frank Zappa and the Red Hot Chili Peppers, as well as a *TIME* magazine cover. In 2005 he designed a line of clothing for the Japanese company A Bathing Ape.

He was head designer of *Pee-wee's Playhouse,* for which he won three Emmy Awards.

In 2000, Gary was awarded a Chrysler Design Award. Since 2001 he has been collaborating with Joshua White (of the Joshua Light Show) on experimental lightshows. He is represented by Dunn & Brown Gallery in Dallas. A two-volume monograph of his work was published in 2008 by Picturebox.

- For many years *Dal Tokyo,* the comic strip, has been appearing in a monthly Japanese reggae magazine called *Riddim.* Dal Tokyo is a fantasy world I began inventing in 1974 where most of my comic creations still wander.

The idea is that in a few hundred years Mars will have been inhabited by various combinations of earthly cultures. My fantasy centers on the idea of a Japanese and Texan colony on Mars and the possible cultural mix-ups that might result.

Of course this fantasy is not likely to look like anything is likely to look like on Mars in the future, but that is beside the point. As an artistic temper I can design my little world any way I want—it is my private sandbox and there I am king for a while. I try to make it wondrous somehow. Anyway I can. I wonder about it and worry it into life. I get energy out of the device.

Laura Park was born in 1980 in southern California. As a child she drew constantly and was so clumsy it's a wonder she has functioning kneecaps and her original teeth. Currently she is contributing comics to *Mome* and compiling a book of her sketchbook comics.

- This story was created for *Adhouse Books' Superior Showcase,* an anthology of comics with a superhero theme. Superhero stories remind me of the childhood I spent reading them, so this piece is loosely autobiographical.

Mimi Pond was born and raised in San Diego, California, and attended the California College of Arts and Crafts in Oakland, California, for three years. Following that, she moved down the street to work as a waitress Mama's Royal Cafe, where she often told customers that her job there was her graduate work.

And they believed her.

After four years there she moved to New York to pursue a career as a cartoonist and illustrator. Her work appeared in countless publications, from the *Village Voice* to the *New York Times.*

After eight years in New York, she and her husband, the painter Wayne White, moved to Los Angeles. There they are raising two very talented artists, Lulu and Woodrow White, and Mimi continues to publish cartoons regularly in the Sunday opinion pages of the *Los Angeles Times*.

▪ "Over Easy" is a fictionalized memoir about my waitressing career in Oakland, California, in the late '70s and early '80s. Set against the backdrop of the burgeoning punk scene of the Bay Area, the restaurant was awash in sex, drugs, and enough attitude to make short-order cooks and waitresses think they were all Sid and Nancy. From my very first shift, I knew it was a story. I just didn't count on it taking thirty years to all come together. The soundtrack for the major motion picture made from this story would have to include, at the very least, Jonathan Richman's "I Have Come Out to Play," Elvis Costello's "Welcome to the Working Week," and Nick Lowe's "Half a Boy and Half a Man."

Ron Regé Jr. lives and works in Los Angeles, where he also creates music in the band Lavender Diamond.

▪ "Cruddy: Chapter 8" was originally created for the zine *Lo-Jinx*. The theme of the issue involved cartoonists creating work in the style of other cartoonists, mostly in a satirical way. I chose to create a comic strip out of some prose work by Lynda Barry. Lynda's comics often contain a large amount of narration. I decided therefore, as an exercise, to use none at all. It was a lot of fun, and it greatly affected the way that I now approach the idea of adapting written work into the "comics" format.

David Sandlin was born in 1956 in Belfast, Northern Ireland, and raised on a diet of potatoes, cabbage, and American horror comics sneaked from his mother's stash. He spent an inordinate portion of his early youth drawing goofy monsters inspired by *Mad* and Jack Kirby before Belfast's daily bombings precipitated his family's move to rural Alabama in the early '70s. Reeling with culture shock from which he has yet to recover, he moved to New York City in 1980, where he's lived ever since. He recently completed volume seven of *A Sinner's Progress*, a series of narrative artist's books that range from hand-silkscreened editions to a Fantagraphic-printed pulp-style comic. He teaches at the School of Visual Arts and publishes his work whenever and wherever he's asked, including in *RAW, Snake Eyes, Strapazin, Blab!, The Ganzfeld,* and *Hotwire.*

▪ The pages contributed in this anthology are from a larger silkscreened book I did, called *Slumburbia*, the latest of my Sinner's Progress series, and it was also printed in *Hotwire II* in 2008. A meditation on sloth, indolence, and lust (an inevitable theme in all my work), it's part of my ongoing obsession about American culture's schizophrenic puritanism. I love to paint and do a lot of it, but I think of myself primarily as a printmaker with strong narrative propensities; I'm inspired by comics, and it's just natural to me that I make them. I love the democratic nature of the medium and the forum it gives me, and I'm always thrilled to be included in the realm of comics and graphic narrative.

Koren Shadmi was born in Israel, where he has worked since his early teens as an illustrator and cartoonist for various magazines. When he was seventeen, he had his first graphic novel published, followed by another book collecting his work from children's magazines. He then served as a graphic designer and illustrator in the Israeli Defense Force. Upon completion of his service he relocated to New York to study at the School of Visual Arts, where he earned his bachelor's degree.

His graphic work has appeared in numerous international anthologies, and his books have been published in France, Italy, and the United States. Koren's illustration work has appeared in publications such as *Spin, BusinessWeek, The Village Voice,* the *Boston Globe,* the *New York Times,* the *Progressive,* the *San Francisco Chronicle,* and many others. He lives and works in Brooklyn.

▪ "Antoinette" deals—like many of my stories—with incomplete and unfulfilled connections between two people. Our guy does not for a moment mention or notice that his beloved is decapitated; it is as if he needs to get to know her in person to realize that she is not quite right. I think on some level the story shows how irrational an infatuation can be, and how it may sometimes lead to a "disembodied" and incomplete relationship.

Dash Shaw is the cartoonist of a few different books, most recently *The Bottomless Belly Button* from Fantagraphics Books in 2008, and his Web comic, "BodyWorld," which will be collected in book form by Pantheon Books in 2010. He is also a regular contributor to *Mome*, the Fantagraphics quarterly anthology where "The Galactic Funnels" originally appeared. Visit www.dashshaw.com for more information, comics, and animations.

▪ This is a dense allegorical story that brushes against a bunch of ideas in a pretty immature, pissy way, rather than exploring anything fully. One good thing about it is that I felt like I came out the other end grown intellectually and emotionally somehow. Sometimes I finish a short story and I feel like the only thing that happened between when I started it and when I finished it was that I'd learned a new way to draw or color or sequence something—technical things. Or I just realize that I don't want to do another comic like whatever I did. That's fine with me, but ideally every comic would push me forward as a person, rather than just as a cartoonist. This comic is strange in that I've noticed other cartoonists like it a lot, but all of the "normal" people who've read it (my family and noncartoonist friends) don't like it.

▪ Perhaps best known for his masterful Holocaust narratives *Maus* and *Maus II*—which in 1992 won a Pulitzer Prize—**Art Spiegelman** is one of the world's best known and beloved comic artists. At the same time as he was publishing his comics, Spiegelman worked as a creative consultant for Topps Candy from 1965 to 1987, designing Wacky Packages, Garbage Pail Kids, and other novelty items, and he taught history and aesthetics of comics at the School for Visual Arts in New York from 1979 to 1986. In 1980, Spiegelman founded *RAW*, the acclaimed avant-garde comics magazine, with his wife, Françoise Mouly. His work has since been published in many periodicals, including *The New Yorker*, where he was a staff artist and writer from 1993 to 2003. Spiegelman is the author, most recently, of *Breakdowns* (Pantheon), *Jack and the Box* (Toon Books), and a bound package of three sketchbooks titled *Be a Nose! Be a Nose!* (McSweeney's). He is the recipient of a Guggenheim fellowship, and, in addition to winning the Pulitzer Prize, *Maus* was nominated for a National Book Critics' Circle Award. His drawings and prints have been widely exhibited here and abroad. He lives in New York City with his wife and their two children.

▪ When Dan Frank, my editor at Pantheon, expressed interest in republishing *Breakdowns*, I figured I'd write some sort of brief introduction—memories and notions that shaped me as a cartoonist . . . But then to make my life more complicated I decided to do it in comix form and it ended up being almost as long as the book it was introducing. This "Portrait of the Artist as a Young %@#*!!" sequence, portions of which were serialized in the *Virginia Quarterly Review*, is part of that introduction.

Ted Stearn earned his BFA at the Rhode Island School of Design, and an MFA at the School of Visual Arts in New York. He has been drawing comics whenever he gets a chance to for the past sixteen years, notably his endless *Fuzz & Pluck* series, published by Fantagraphics Books. Ted's checkered experiences have taken him to all corners of the world of visual arts: painting, sculpture, illustration, and graphic design. But he has earned his bread and butter mostly as a storyboard artist for animation. He has also taught comics and storyboarding at the Savannah College of Art and Design. Ted currently lives in Los Angeles.

▪ The twenty pages selected for this book are an excerpt from Fuzz and Pluck in *Splitsville #5*. The entire series has recently been collected in the book *Fuzz & Pluck: Splitsville* from Fantagraphics Books. The central characters are Fuzz, a teddy bear, and Pluck, a denuded chicken. Although Fuzz and Pluck first met in a garbage truck, their adventures have no beginning and no end (in an old-fashioned comics way). I originally dreamed up Fuzz and Pluck from some inane doodles in a desperate attempt to meet a deadline way back in 1993. Little did I realize how far they would take me. Perhaps they have lasted for so long because (in hindsight) I noticed Fuzz reflects the child in me and Pluck reflects the adult in me. Security and survival are their motivation, just as in my life. And as in life, these two paradigms seem incomplete without each other.

Jillian Tamaki grew up in the Canadian prairies but now lives in Brooklyn, New York. She has been illustrating since 2003, when she graduated from the Alberta College of Art and Design with a bachelor's degree in design. Her clients include the *New York Times, The New Yorker,* the *Washington Post, Esquire, SPIN,* Penguin Canada, and the Canadian Broadcasting Company. Awards include gold medals from the Society of Illustrators and the Society of Publication Designers. Conundrum Press (Montreal) released *Gilded Lilies,* a small book of mini-comics and drawings, in 2006. Jillian began teaching in the illustration department at the Parsons School of Design in the fall of 2007. Visit her at www.jilliantamaki.com.

Mariko Tamaki is a writer from Toronto, Ontario. Her previous published works include *Cover Me, True Lies: The Book of Bad Advice,* and *Fake ID.* Mariko is also the writer of the graphic novel *Emiko Superstar,* illustrated by Steve Rolston. Her work has appeared in a variety of Canadian newspapers and magazines. When she is not writing, Mariko is teaching, mostly creative writing, mostly to crazy high school students who come up with the weirdest stuff when prompted with a blank piece of paper, a pen, and some mild threats.

Skim was voted the Best of 2008 by *Publishers Weekly* and one of the top ten children's illustrated books by the *New York Times.* It was nominated for the Canadian Governor General's Award for Children's Literature, and received the Ignatz in 2008 for Best Graphic Novel.

▪ *Jillian:* Our process of creating *Skim* was organic but not back-and-forth. *Skim* came to me as a fully realized "script" and what I came back with a few months later was a rough version that closely resembled the finished product. We both added our contributions at different parts of the process. This project allowed me to really explore the possibilities of storytelling visually, especially through details, expressions, and unspoken movements. It ended up creating another dimension to the character and the concept of a diary. There is an incongruity between what is said and what is felt.

▪ *Mariko:* My original idea was to create a gothic, queer Lolita story. What came out as I started writing was all this other stuff I wanted to say about being a teenager, about how big ideas and big dramas mix together with the petty ridiculousness of everyday life. One of my favorite scenes in this book is the fight between Skim and Lisa in the school bathroom. I really enjoyed writing the dialogue between these two characters. I love how Jillian's illustrations add silences to this interaction, extra meaning with the stone expressions on the characters' faces. The best part of writing this book was watching Jillian take the text and create this whole tableau with it. I'd never had the chance to see a story come alive in that particular way before. It's pretty awesome.

Adrian Tomine was born in 1974 in Sacramento, California. He is the writer/artist of the comic book series *Optic Nerve,* and also serves as editor and designer for the English-language editions of the comics of Yoshihiro Tatsumi (published by Drawn & Quarterly). His illustrations appear with some regularity in *The New Yorker.* His contribution to this anthology is an excerpt from his graphic novel *Shortcomings,* the paperback edition of which was recently published by Drawn & Quarterly. He lives in Brooklyn and is presently at work on a new, untitled book.

▪ This story developed as a reaction against an element that I saw in my previous work: namely, the desire on my part to be somehow "liked" on a personal level by some hypothetical reader. I'm not sure how successful I was, but I was trying to free myself of the self-censorship that comes from that mindset, and I also just wanted to create an entertaining, fictional story and maybe find a use for some dumb, off-color jokes I'd accumulated in my brain.

Chris Ware is the author of *Jimmy Corrigan — The Smartest Kid on Earth* and the annual amateur periodical *The ACME Novelty Library*. A contributor to *The New Yorker* and the *Virginia Quarterly Review*, Mr. Ware was the first cartoonist chosen to regularly serialize an ongoing story in the *New York Times Magazine* in 2005 and 2006. He edited the thirteenth issue of *McSweeney's Quarterly Concern* in 2004 as well as Houghton Mifflin's *Best American Comics 2007*, and his work was the focus of an exhibit at the Museum of Contemporary Art in Chicago in 2006 and the Sheldon Memorial Art Gallery in Lincoln, Nebraska, in 2007. Mr. Ware lives in Oak Park, Illinois, with his wife, Marnie, a high school science teacher, and their daughter, Clara.

▪ Operating under the conceit of one moment per year per page representing one person's life, the person and life in question here are that of Jordan Wellington Lint, b. 1958, and the moments selected fall between 1983 and 1990. Rendered motherless as a tot and friendless as a teen, in this excerpt Jordan has just come to the end of a father-funded bid as a music producer in Los Angeles and is refusing to return to his hometown of Omaha, Nebraska, lest he be considered an embarrassing failure. He does, however, return, and to his surprise finds happiness, trust, and love there in a woman who, by the end of the selection, becomes his wife. These pages contribute to the in-progress graphic novel *Rusty Brown* and have appeared in the *Virginia Quarterly Review* by the good and tolerant graces of the editor there, Ted Genoways, who is, like myself, a transplanted Nebraskan.

Dan Zettwoch was born in Louisville, Kentucky, in 1977. His earliest artistic influences were his father Donald "Toots" Zettwoch, grandfather Dalton "Wet Sock" Zettwoch, the host of the PBS kids' drawing show "Commander" Mark Kistler, Ed Emberley, the Usual Gang of Idiots at *Mad*, and whoever drew the short-lived Marvel motocross comic *Team America*. He moved to St. Louis, Missouri, to study at Washington University and continues to live and work there, making comics, illustrations, prints, and how-to diagrams. In addition to several self-published booklets, his stories have appeared in *Kramers Ergot*, the *Drawn & Quarterly Showcase*, *Nickelodeon*, and Yale University Press's *An Anthology of Graphic Fiction, Cartoons, and True Stories Volume 2*. He is currently working on the weekly newspaper strip *Amazing Facts & Beyond* with fellow USS Catastrophe crew members Kevin Huizenga and Ted May, and his own book, *Redbird*.

▪ I was raised around antique machinery, professional wrestling, raunchy homemade cartoons, slow-pitch softball, and the Episcopal Church. When I was asked to draw a strip for *Comic Art Magazine* — the great journal of comics history and criticism — I wanted to make something that captured several small moments in the nuts-and-bolts history of comic reproduction, but also the accidental history of a midwestern church and its staff artist, my (fictional) uncle Darryl. "Spirit Duplicator: Selected Church Bulletin Comics of Darryl Zettwoch 1968–1998" is my attempt to do that.

Notable Comics

from September 1, 2007, to August 31, 2008

Selected by Jessica Abel and Matt Madden

TREVOR ALIXOPOULOS
  The Hot Breath of War, 2008.
KATE ALLEN
  Milk-Teeth, 2008.
LYNDA BARRY
  What It Is, 2008.
RICHARD BEARDS
  Shapes of Things. *Blab!*, no. 18.
MIKE BERTINO
  Pinwheel, 2008.
STEVE BISETTE
  Secrets & Lies, Windows & Wounds. *Secrets and Lies*, no. 7.
AARON COSTAIN
  Entropy Part 2, 2008.
JOSHUA COTTER
  Skyscrapers of the Midwest, 2008.
KEN DAHL
  Gordon Smalls Hurts Himself. *Welcome to the Dahl House*, 2008.
MIKE DAWSON
  Freddie & Me: A Coming-of-Age (Bohemian) Rhapsody, 2008.
HILARY FLORIDO
  I Love Love (Too Bad I Hate You), 2008.
SEAN FORD
  Only Skin, no. 2.
  Only Skin, no. 3.
CHARLES FORSMAN
  Snake Oil, no. 1.
  Snake Oil, no. 2.
ALEXIS FREDERICK-FROST
  Letter. *3 Stories*, 2008.

DEREK VAN GIESEN
  Parallelogram. *Mome*, Fall 2008.
SARAH GLIDDEN
  How to Understand Israel in 60 Days or Less, 2007.
MICHEL GONDRY
  We Lost the War But Not the Battle, 2008.
NICHOLAS GUREWITCH
  The Trial of Colonel Sweeto and Other Stories, 2007.
JAIME HERNANDEZ
  Ti-Girls Adventures Number 34. *Love and Rockets: New Stories*, no. 1.
HOB
  The Witness: A Ghost Story, 2008.
ALEX HOLDEN
  Magic Hour Sketchbook, 2008.
JOE INFURNARI
  The Process, 2008.
R. KIKUO JOHNSON AND A.E. STALLINGS
  Recitative. *The Poem as Comic Strip*, no. 6.
TOM KACZYNSKI
  Million Year Boom. *Mome*, Summer 2008.
MARTHA KEAVNEY
  Cease & Desist. *Spelt-Rite Comics*, no. 1
  The Minuscules. *Spelt-Rite Comics*, no. 1
JAMES KOCHALKA
  American Elf. www.americanelf.com.
PETER KUPER
  Bully for You. *Blab!*, no. 18.
JOSEPH LAMBERT
  Untitled (Dinosaurs-Caveman), 2008.
TIM LANE
  Outing. *Abandoned Cars*, 2008.

HOPE LARSON/BRYAN LEE O'MALLEY
Bear Creek Apartments. www.radiomaru.com, 2008.

JUSTIN MADSON
Breathers, no. 1.
Breathers, no. 2.

LARS MARTINSON
Tōnoharu: Part One, 2008.

BRIAN MARUCA AND JIM RUGG
Street Angel. *Superior Showcase*, no. 3.

ANDREI MOLOTIU
Expedition to the Interior. *Blurred Vision*, no. 4.

CORINNE MUCHA
Shithole, 2008.

NATE NEAL
Reality Comics Quartet. *Mome*, Fall 2008.

SARAH OLEKSYK
Fifteen Variations on "The First Day We Met." *Nerd Burglar*, 2008.

BRYAN LEE O'MALLEY
Scott Pilgrim Gets It Together, 2007.

CHRIS ONSTAD
Achewood. www.achewood.com.

JOHN PORCELLINO
88th and Federal. *King-Cat Comics*, no. 68.
Thoreau at Walden, 2008.

MICHEL RABAGLIATI
Paul Goes Fishing, 2008.

JOAN REILLY
Hank and Barbara. www.smithmag.net, May 2008.

JESSE REKLAW
Slow Wave. www.slowwave.com.

STAN SAKAI
Usagi Yojimbo Volume 22: Tomoe's Story, 2008.

FRANK SANTORO
STOREYVILLE, 2007.

FRANK SANTORO AND JIM RUGG
Cold Heat: Special 4, 2008.

SAM SHARPE
Return Me to the Sea, 2008.

DASH SHAW
Look Forward, First Son of Terra Two. *Mome*, Winter/Spring 2008.
Bottomless Belly Button, 2008.

JEFF SMITH
Rasl, no. 1.
Rasl, no. 2.

JOSHUA RAY STEPHENS
The Moth or the Flame, 2008.

JAMES STOKOE
Wonton Soup, 2007.

JAMES STURM AND RICH TOMMASO
Satchel Paige: Striking Out Jim Crow, 2007.

JAMIE TANNER
There Once Was a Girl . . ., 2008.

LAUREN WEINSTEIN
Goddess of War, 2008.

SKIP WILLIAMSON
Daddy Was a Lady. *Blab!*, no. 18.

CALVIN WONG
Hattie et Millie, 2008.

JEFF ZWIREK
Burning Building Comix, no. 2.